MW00565396
LEADING
LITERATE
LIVES

LEADING LITERATE LIVES

Habits and Mindsets for Reimagining Classroom Practice

Stephanie Affinito

HEINEMANN
Portsmouth, NH

Heinemann
361 Hanover Street
Portsmouth, NH 03801–3912
www.heinemann.com

Offices and agents throughout the world

The author and publisher wish to thank those who have generously given permission to reprint borrowed material:

RAN chart by Anthony Stead. Copyright © 2012 by Anthony Stead. Reprinted with permission from the author.

Numbered list from "5 Steps to Build a Diverse Classroom Library and Encourage Empathy" by Jennifer Williams, as first appeared in *Education Week*'s Global Learning on September 6, 2017: www.edweek.org/teaching-learning/opinion-5-steps-to-build-a-diverse-classroom-library-and-encourage-empathy/2017/09. Reprinted with permission from the author.

Figure 3.3 created with Padlet: https://padlet.com/. Reprinted with permission from the website.

Numbered list adapted from *Hidden Gems: Naming and Teaching from the Brilliance in Every Student's Writing* by Katherine Bomer. Copyright © 2010 by Katherine Bomer. Published by Heinemann. Reprinted with permission from the publisher.

Library of Congress Control Number: 2021902656
ISBN: 978-0-325-11832-1

Editor: Holly Kim Price
Production: Victoria Merecki
Cover design: Monica Ann Cohen
Cover image: © Irbena / Shutterstock
Author photo: Kemm Wilson
Text design: Monica Ann Cohen and Susan Godel
Typesetter: Shawn Girsberger
Manufacturing: Val Cooper

Printed in the United States of America on acid-free paper
1 2 3 4 5 VP 26 25 24 23 22 21
February 2021 Printing

To my family:

I wouldn't be the kind of reader and writer

I am today without you.

To educators everywhere making reading

and writing a daily part of their lives:

Thank you for your continued inspiration.

CONTENTS

ACKNOWLEDGMENTS

Readers and writers are built one page at a time, and I'm so thankful for the people in my life who have been part of my reading and writing journey.

To my dad: All those magical hours spent in the library had a tremendous impact on my life. Thank you for setting me on the path to becoming a reader—and a writer.

To my mom: Those long days spent at home filled with conversation, hours of reading, and lots of journal writing sparked the kind of literate life I have today.

To my grandparents: Thank you for the countless trips to the library, the mad dashes to the bookstore when the newest Babysitters Club book arrived, and the personalized writing paper that made me believe my words mattered.

To my husband and children: Thank you for the treasured memories of reading and writing together—and for putting up with my stacks of books and journals everywhere.

To my colleagues and students at the University at Albany: Thank you for your dedication to lifelong learning and our partnerships around reading and writing.

To the extraordinary Heinemann team: Thank you for believing in my work once again. I am constantly in awe of the dedication each one of you brings to teachers and their students.

To my editor, Holly: Words cannot express my gratitude for growing a seed idea into the book it is today. I'm so thankful for our work together.

To my fellow educators, readers, and writers: Thank you for being part of my literate journey. There aren't enough pages to adequately thank everyone who has impacted my literate life, but I would like to acknowledge a special few: Kris McGee, for your friendship, book dealing, and #BookYourself; Shelley Fenton, Krista Senatore, and Logan Fisher, for the countless book recommendations and notebooking inspiration; Jen Laffin and Michelle Haseltine, for #TeachWrite and #100DaysofNotebooking; Brenda Power and Ruth Ayres, for the Choice Literacy writing community and Two Writing Teachers, and the Nerdy Book Club for their daily blogging inspiration from afar. I cherish these connections.

To authors everywhere: Thank you for showing up to the page. This book would not be possible without you.

INTRODUCTION

Cultivate What Matters Most

I adore stories. As a child, I devoured them, vicariously living through the characters I met in the pages of a book. As a teenager, I wrote them, using writing as a way to work through the turbulence of adolescence. As an adult, I live them and feel the power these lived stories have to shape my identity. And as an educator, I value them and respect the role our unique stories have in shaping teaching and learning.

If I think back on my career as a learner, I can clearly remember the teachers who became part of my story. Some of my experiences with teachers were positive: my first-grade teacher who joyfully came to school each day ready to learn with us; my sixth-grade teacher who reminded me that school was not just about academic learning but also about forging connections with others; my college professor who pushed my thinking and challenged my practices, reminding me that there was always something new to consider. Some of the experiences were negative: my kindergarten teacher who would leave the room because we were not behaving properly, leaving us wondering whether she'd ever return;

my high-school teacher who focused on getting things right over the process of learning; my college professor who would return my papers covered in red pen with a message to find writing help somewhere, but not in class. Each of these stories, along with countless others, have played a role in shaping the kind of person and educator I am today.

As educators, we strive to shape students' stories in positive ways, engaging students' hearts and minds through the work we do. We want students to feel welcomed, valued, and respected. We want them to know they matter and that we believe in their abilities, even those they do not yet know they possess. We want students to feel the power that literacy has to change their view of themselves and their world and then feel confident enough to share their voices and stories with others. But sometimes, we shape students' stories by the decisions we make in the midst of the challenges we face as educators, decisions that have unintended consequences for our students' stories: when we struggle to find space in the curriculum for students' questions, when we frame reading and writing as work, or when we privilege getting things done over learning about ourselves. These practices can quietly seep into our classrooms and, over time, can even become the norm and inadvertently shape students' ideas of what literacy learning is and could be. These unintentional messages hold great power in shaping our students' stories, but it can be incredibly difficult to acknowledge their presence. It is only when we approach our classroom through the lens of a learner that we can truly experience what matters most to the minds and hearts of our students. And, upon reflection, we may find that our classroom practices do not reflect what we would advocate for ourselves.

A while back, I was working with a group of teachers who wanted to explore reading and reading response in their classrooms. A traditional model of professional learning would call for a session to highlight research on best practices, provide examples for what teachers might try in their classrooms, and offer classroom coaching as an additional support. But I didn't do that. Instead, I engaged teachers as readers themselves, readers who came together in a community to respond to texts. We formed a book club, read new and diverse texts, and responded to our reading in multiple ways. I gave book talks on titles the teachers might be interested in reading. We read anchor texts together and had rich conversations about our reading. We chose individual titles and eagerly book-talked our selections. We created reading responses that grew from our experiences: some participants placed sticky notes on the pages, some jotted their thoughts in a notebook, some went digital, and others shared their thinking in a discussion. In short, we reconnected with our lives as readers and formed a reading community full of joyful reading—and it changed everything.

As we ended our reading of *Refugee* by Alan Gratz, we grappled with our emotions. How could we accurately capture the incredibly personal and emotional responses that we were having as we read this book? How could we capture our shock at the events these children experienced while we were nicely snuggled into our safe corners of town? How were we going to deal with the discomfort of knowing that these experiences are currently happening? Deciding how to respond to the book was a difficult decision; so, rather than respond back to the book, we thought forward. We investigated our family histories and shared our learning. We gathered articles from local newspapers and media sites on related events happening in our hometowns. We shared lists of unanswered questions we felt compelled to investigate.

Most importantly, we questioned our classroom practices as a result: Do we bring powerful books like this into our classrooms to spark deep thinking about the world our students are living in today? Do we give students opportunities to share their reading with others without worrying about right or wrong answers? Do we all allow students choice in how they respond to their reading based on the transaction they had with the author? Do we allow students to think forward, or do we continually require a response back instead? We even dared to ask whether we ever let students simply sit with their thinking and not respond at all. The very practices we gave ourselves the luxury of indulging in were not always evident in our classrooms. And because we lived as readers and experienced these lessons for ourselves, we couldn't help but feel compelled to rethink our classroom practices.

These kinds of lived experiences help us develop a deeper understanding of learning and what it means to be readers and writers. Reconnecting with our literate lives reminded us of what was most important, brought greater intention and joy to our work, and compelled us to reimagine our stories of teaching and learning in our classrooms. And this kind of work has the potential to change students' lives.

What if we imagine a story where we cultivate our lives as readers, writers, and learners together? A story of reading communities that privilege interest over levels and favor transactions over artifacts, and in which our reading identities hold just as much weight as our reading skills. A story of writing instruction where process is valued over product, creativity comes before uniformity, and the message is more important than the convention. A story of learning where we remain curious as learners and where inquiry leads our learning, choice trumps mandates, and joy permeates the threads of the classroom.

When we reconnect with our lives as readers and writers, we gain a deeper understanding about the messages our practices send to students. Sometimes, our practices are validated as we renew our own commitment to powerful literacy instruction. Sometimes, they are questioned as we uncover a mismatch between what we believe and live as learners and what is evident in our schools and classrooms. Either way, we emerge with a sense of collective responsibility to renew our teaching with authenticity, intention, and joy in order to better impact students' literate stories of themselves. This work begins with us.

I invite you to honor and indulge your own reading and writing life, to outgrow yourself as a reader and writer, and to imagine new possibilities for your literate life and the literate community in your classroom. This book will walk you through the steps to reclaim *your* reading and writing and to bring a new level of awareness to your classroom. You might encounter familiar practices in which you already engage. You might encounter practices you have heard about but have not yet tried in your own literate life. And, you'll likely find practices to boost your reading and writing life in new ways. While this book could be read cover to cover, revealing carefully stacked practices to reconnect as readers and writers, it was designed for readers to choose their own path based on their unique literacy journey.

We begin by uncovering our histories as learners and reflect on our reading and writing lives. It might be tempting to skip this step of the process or to give it less time than it deserves, but please don't. This reflection is a very necessary part of the process to reconnect with ourselves and gain greater insight into our practices. Then, you'll learn about a framework for tending to your literate identity and explore how to nourish your literate habits, hearts, and communities and sustain them over time. You'll read and write your way to a more fulfilled literate life and bring a newfound energy to your classroom. You'll find concrete ideas to replicate the very invitations that impact your own reading and writing with students and likely be inspired to transform your teaching based on your own experiences as a reader and writer.

You'll also find specific tools and activities to rekindle your relationship with your literate life. There are two main sections to this book: reading and writing. Each section is divided into three chapters: habits, hearts, and communities. Setting your own goals as a reader and writer, you'll read, write, and pay close attention to what you learn about yourself in the process. You'll create authentic examples of your learning to share with students, reflect on your instructional practices, and imagine new possibilities for teaching and learning in your classroom and school. I recommend using a notebook to capture your reading and writing reflections. My own notebook is a simple bound journal with blank pages, but you'll want to choose a journal that works for you.

Each chapter offers specific prompts for reflection: What conditions mattered most to our own learning? Which practices supported our efforts and which hindered them? What lessons did we learn as we lived as learners? How might these ideas manifest in our classroom? This kind of intentional self-reflection can be hard to come by in our busy lives as educators, but it is essential if we are to learn from our own experiences as learners. Then, propelled by the exhilaration we often feel when we uncover important realizations about our practice, we'll begin to imagine new possibilities for our classrooms: changes to daily routines, instructional practices, the materials we privilege, and/or how we bring our students' voices into our learning. You'll find ideas to spark your own thinking as well as clear examples of how teachers reimagined their classroom practices as a result of their own learning. While these invitations have been carefully designed to fuel your own literate life, you'll find that they are perfect to replicate with your students as you build your literate lives together.

As educators, it is our responsibility to live as learners: to read, write, think, and learn alongside our students and to imagine a learning community that is better than it was the day before. And, fueled with the understandings that can only come from being learners ourselves, we can ensure that our teaching cultivates what matters most and brings greater intention and joy to our classrooms.

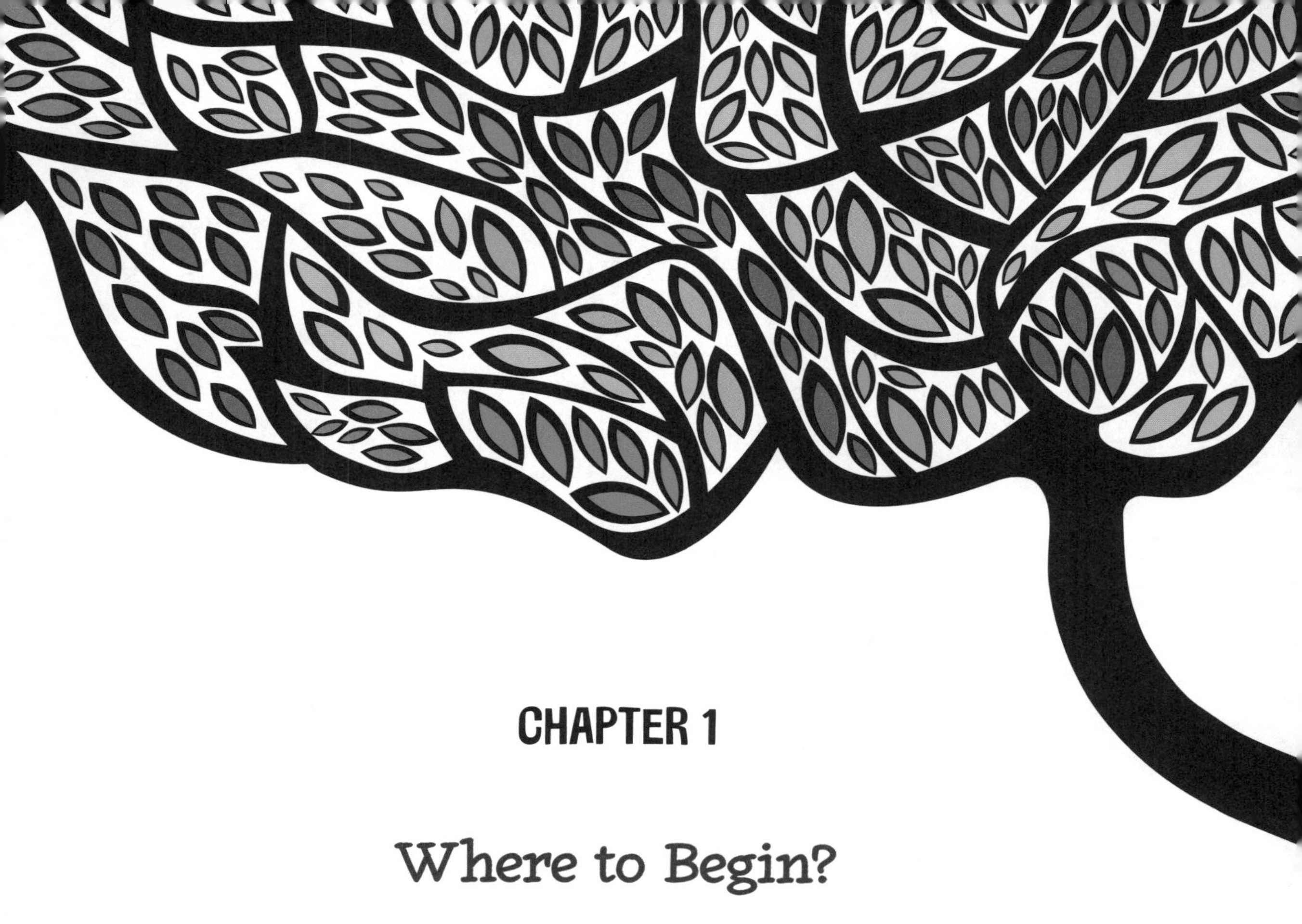

CHAPTER 1

Where to Begin?

Merriam-Webster (2020d) defines *reflection* as "a thought, idea, or opinion formed or a remark made as a result of meditation; consideration of some subject matter, idea, or purpose; and the production of an image by or as if by a mirror." Essentially, reflection is the act of looking inward and taking time to reflect on our thinking and practice as educators. We can trace the role of reflection in education back to Dewey (1933), who believed that reflection was essential for learning from experience. He introduced reflection as a way for teachers to link prior knowledge with current experience to gain a greater understanding of their practices and improve classroom learning. Donald Schön (1987) extended this work through his idea of reflective practice where teachers thoughtfully consider their own experiences in relation to their practices to better understand their unique teaching style and increase their effectiveness.

Why is reflection and reflective practice important to our work as teachers? Here are some important benefits:

- Reflection embodies an inquiry approach to teaching and learning and invites teachers to learn from and about their own practices.
- Reflection helps teachers think deliberately and intentionally about how their teaching decisions impact student learning.
- Regular reflection helps teachers avoid snap, reactive decisions in challenging situations and make thoughtful and intentional decisions instead.
- Reflective teachers model mindsets and practices for students, helping them become reflective learners.
- Reflection can lead to greater insight of our strengths and needs as teachers, leading to better self-care.

There is no single right way to reflect. You might simply be still with yourself at the end of the day and think inwardly. You might capture your daily thinking in a calendar or agenda. You might write or sketch your thoughts in a journal. You might even record your thinking through photographs, audio clips, or video clips. Regardless of the method, reflecting on our practice helps us make instructional decisions that positively impact students.

In my experience, the most common form of reflection parallels the instructional cycle in the classroom: we celebrate what is going well, think critically about the lessons we learned when things didn't, and choose goals for the future. This kind of instructional reflection brings clarity to our thinking, insight to our instruction, and relevance to our goals as teachers. But, sometimes, it can be difficult to see what is right in front of our eyes but outside of our own experiences and assumptions. Therefore, we must approach reflection through a critically reflective lens (Brookfield 1995): by reflecting both on our experiences as learners and through the lens of our students, we can think more clearly about our practices and the messages they may inadvertently send.

Return to Our Roots

Research shows that our learning histories and teaching philosophies influence both our instructional actions within the classroom (Cole and Knowles 2000) and our expectations of students (Dozier 2006), but these influences aren't always conscious or clear. Take a moment to think about how your history as a learner might impact the teaching decisions you make today:

- What does independent reading look like and sound like in your classroom? Is your classroom quiet, or is there a hum or buzz? Are students at their seats, or can they roam the room? Can they read freely, or are there particular requirements about book choice and reading response?
- What genres of writing do your students gravitate toward? Do they prefer fiction over nonfiction? Do they love or loathe poetry? What does the revision and editing process look like?
- How do students share their learning with others? Do they respond to required assignments, or do they have creative freedom to choose a format that works best for them? Do they rely on paper and pencil, or can they use technology to capture their thinking?
- What opportunities abound for creative making in your classroom? Do students have the freedom to tinker? Can they explore manipulatives to spark creativity or enhance the learning process? Or are they restricted to a set of curricular resources instead?

Some of our responses to these questions might be the result of school structures, required curriculum, and formal assessments that decide what we privilege in the classroom. But some of our responses might be connected to what we have experienced and prefer as learners. Do you prefer a quiet reading environment and thus prefer the same for your classroom? Do you hang onto the belief that students must write paper drafts before heading to the computer because that is how you write now or wrote best as a student? Intentional reflection around our own histories and lived experiences as learners is essential if we are going to uncover the why behind our practices and acknowledge the role our experiences play in our classrooms. And here are a few ways to do just that. Choose one (or all!) to return to your roots as a learner and explore how your own experiences might impact your current classroom.

Draw Readers and/or Writers

A drawing activity based on Kaback's (2016) informal "draw-a-reader" assessment provides compelling insight into our identities as readers and writers and is a creative way to represent our thinking. Here's how it works:

Draw a quick sketch of what a reader and/or writer is to you. Think about where, how, and why readers read and/or writers write. Think about the ways readers and/or writers look and feel, and make your drawing as detailed as possible. Supplement your drawing with text, writing words and phrases that come to mind when you think about what it means to be a reader and/or writer. Once you've completed your annotated drawing, reflect on the questions posed in Figure 1.1.

Your drawing is sure to change according to the time of year, the initiatives at your school, your personal life, and more. But right now, what did you learn

Reading	Writing
• What does your image say about your beliefs about reading? • Does your image of a reader match the kind of readerly life you live? • How does reflecting on your image of a reader make you feel and why? • How can this help you think about what your reading life needs next? • How can this help you think about what your classroom reading community needs next?	• What does being a writer mean to you? • Do you meet your personal definition of a writer? Why or why not? • How does reflecting on your personal definition of a writer help you think about what your writing life needs next? • What might you need to rethink about how you define writing and what it means to be a writer? • How can this help you think about your own classroom writing instruction and your students' identities as writers?

FIGURE 1.1 *Reflective questions on what it means to be a reader and writer*

about yourself? How does that help you think about what you need in your reading and writing life?

Create Reading and/or Writing Timelines

Each one of our experiences with reading and writing shapes our literacy beliefs and instruction, and thinking back on our past experiences can give us insight into the kind of readers and writers we are today. Create a timeline of your most memorable reading and/or writing experiences. Start by drawing a timeline grid on a page of your notebook. As you work through the following prompts, add each experience to your timeline, but choose the location based on how it made you feel. Write positive memories above the line and negative memories below it. Or, take a more creative approach, as Lyndsay Buehler did, and create a road map of your reading life instead, with the twists and turns in the road representing the twists and turns in your literate life. You'll find her road map in Figure 1.2.

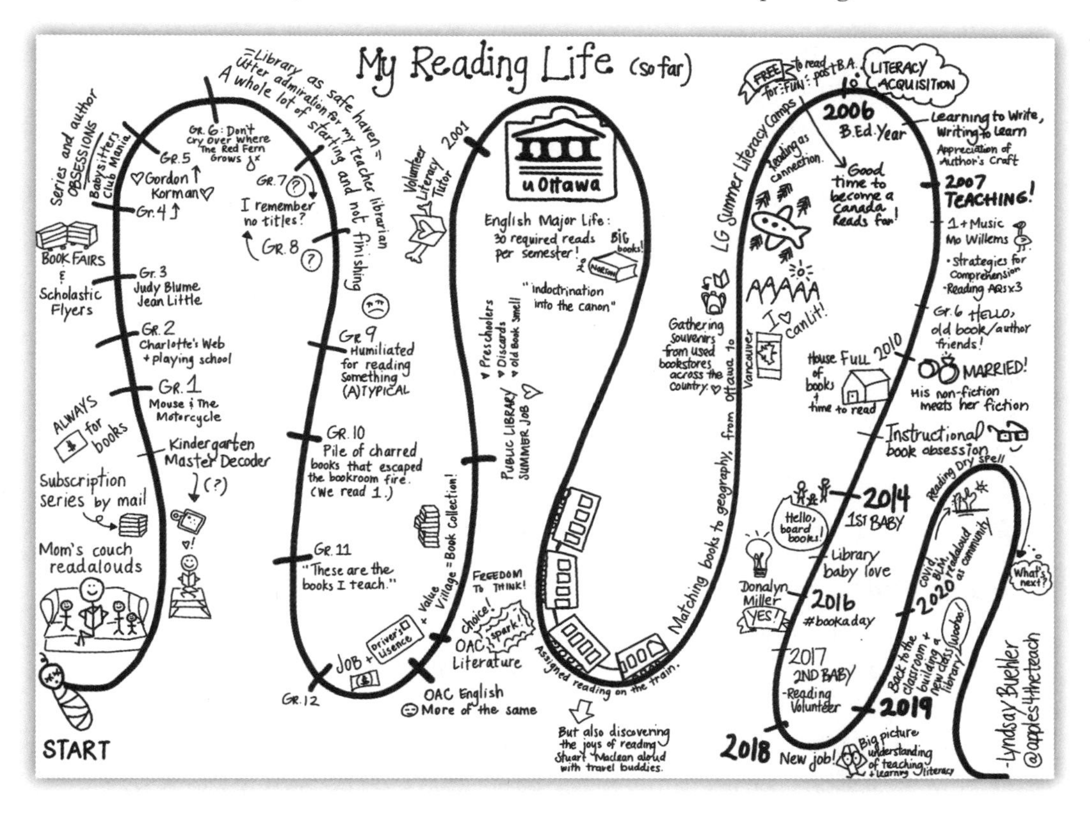

FIGURE 1.2 *Lyndsay Buehler's road map of her reading life*

1. Think back to the earliest memory you have of reading and/or writing. What was it? How old were you? How did it make you feel toward reading/writing? Reflect on your experiences with reading/writing at home. What were they like? Why did you engage with reading/writing? Who supported you? How did you feel? What did reading/writing mean to you? Add your memories to your timeline.
2. Next, think of your experiences in elementary, middle, and high school. What sticks out in your memory, good or bad? Which teachers do you remember making their mark on your reading/writing identity? How might you define reading/writing at this stage of your life? Add your memories to your timeline.
3. Now, think about your college experience and your teacher education program. How did you experience reading/writing as a college student? How did it compare with the kind of reading/writing instruction you learned was best for students? Add your memories to your timeline.
4. What recent experiences have you had with reading/writing? How does your reading/writing life feel? Add your memories to your timeline.

Now, it is time for a bit of reflection. Take a good, long look at your timeline and connect your experiences together with a line, clearly capturing the varied trajectory of your reading/writing life. What do you notice about your timeline? Are there many experiences to reflect on or are your experiences more limited? Are the majority of your memories above the line or do they fall below it? How did your reading/writing life ebb and flow over time? How might each experience contribute to your current reading/writing identity?

Track Your Texts

Books hold a special place in my heart, and particular books have made an indelible impression on my life. My very first memory of reading is when Grover invited me into the pages of his book in *There's a Monster at the End of This Book*. Later, Judy Blume's *Are You There God? It's Me, Margaret* would teach me how the lessons learned through the pages of a book could impact my own life. I devoured Ann M. Martin's The Baby-Sitters Club series throughout my childhood, making clear and lasting connections to the characters and hoping for a tight-knit group of friends for myself. In adulthood, *Gone Girl* and *The Girl on the Train* gave me insight into another side of myself, and *Fifty Shades of Grey,* well, let's say that I was hooked on that series, too. The books we read matter, as each one changes our impression of ourselves and of the world around us.

So, what books matter most to you? Track the texts that have made an impression on you through the years. You might list them on a piece of paper, jot them down in your writer's notebook, or even create a digital collection of book covers. Use the prompts below to help you get started:

- What is the first book you remember being read to you?
- What is the first book you remember reading on your own?
- What books do you remember reading through your childhood? Why were they more memorable over the others?
- Which books helped you work through adolescence? Did any magazines, articles, and media, help you, too?
- What books have you read recently that spoke to your heart? Why do you think so?

It's important not only to think of these titles but also to write them down. You need to *see* them listed to better understand the powerful role they play in your life over time. Now, think about the books you listed. What made them so powerful in your life? Jot those thoughts in your notebook, too.

Archive Your Writing

If you are anything like me, you like to save things: cards; notes from my childhood; old spelling tests with smiley face stickers; the newspapers I "published" as a child; my poems; my childhood diary; mementos from important occasions, such as ticket stubs and flower petals; you get the idea. My basement is filled with clear plastic containers chronicling the life of my three children: their baby calendars, first jar of baby food, tiny socks, and more. I know I may be taking it a bit overboard, but I love holding these mementos in my hand and feeling the waves of emotion come over me.

If you are able to, gather any writing mementos you have from your childhood. You might sift through your own basement for them or call your family members to see if they have anything saved. Holding, touching, and seeing these items can be very powerful, but don't worry if you don't have physical access to them. You can gather them in your mind instead. Why are these items important? How do they represent who you are as a writer? How do they make you feel? Which are most important and why do they matter? Now, think about your current writing life. How does it compare with the kind of writing that matters most to you now? Does the writing you engage in fuel your heart or simply get things done? Are there spaces in your day to create writing artifacts that continue to shape your identity?

Our Literate Habits, Hearts, and Communities

I'll never forget the Friday night I tiptoed into my son's room to give him one last kiss goodnight and could not find him. Instead of seeing him snuggled up in his bed with his blankets, I found him asleep and buried beneath a stack of books with a pack of sticky notes and a marker by his side. As I took a few steps closer, I saw that he had taken the books from his bookshelf, attached each one to a sticky note, and labeled it with a number. As I gently tried to remove the books from his bed, my son woke and shared what he had been doing: he had decided to level his books to see which ones he was allowed to read—and which ones he was not. Now, I knew his teacher was using leveled text during small-group instruction to help students choose good-fit books for independent reading. But the message she inadvertently sent my son about the books he could and could not read had clear implications for his identity as a reader.

These unintentional messages are often the by-product of intentional focus on standards and curriculum. In today's time of heightened standards, mandated curriculum, and the weight of the world bearing down on our classrooms, we might find ourselves focusing on *what* we need to teach rather than the *why* behind the work we do. Understandably, we might focus on skills and standards and create curricular frameworks to ensure we teach them. We might focus on the strategies that our readers and writers must master and create charts and data trails to ensure our students are learning them. We might create lesson guides and protocols to ensure alignment and create pacing guides to support consistency. This work is needed, but it is not enough. We must also focus on the habits that nourish and sustain our reading and writing lives, the practices that set our literate hearts on fire, and the communities we need to learn and grow together. The importance of this heart work becomes much more evident when teachers lead full, nourishing, and satisfying literate lives themselves.

I find it useful to think of the construction of our identities as literate learners in three broad categories: our habits, our hearts, and our communities. You'll find a visual image of this framework in Figure 1.3.

Our Habits:

Choices we make to cultivate our reading and writing lives and make them a priority.

This includes:

- Surrounding ourselves with books and writing tools
- Making time to read and write daily
- Accessing a wide and diverse selection of texts
- Knowing how we read and write best
- Understanding our personal process for writing and how it matters

Our Hearts:

Practices and dispositions that readers and writers embody to bring joy to reading and writing and to fuel their practices.

This includes:

- Learning from writing mentors
- Choosing books and writing formats
- Responding to reading in meaningful ways
- Stretching ourselves as readers and writers
- Setting personal reading and writing goals
- Exploring our reading and writing creativity

Our Communities:

The ways we connect with others to celebrate reading and writing

This includes:

- Making our reading and writing lives visible
- Sharing our reading and writing with others
- Connecting with fellow readers and writers
- Celebrating our literate lives
- Engaging in new learning experiences

FIGURE 1.3 *Our literate habits, hearts, and communities framework*

It is important to note that these categories are not linear or sequential and their format does not imply importance. Nor should we tackle one category at the expense of another. However, I have found comfort in the logical nature of this sequence. If our hope is to boost our learning lives, we must first carve out the time and develop the daily habits needed to do so. Once those habits are firmly in place, we can better honor our literate hearts, reading and writing about what matters most to each of us, and ultimately connect with communities of connected readers and writers working to do the same.

Our Literate Habits

If we want our students to become competent and confident readers and writers, then they consistently need long stretches of time to do what readers and writers do: read, respond to their reading, share books with other readers, gather seed ideas, create lots of false starts, draft, revise and revise again, learn from mentors, connect with reading and writing partners, and, in some cases, publish pieces for particular audiences. But in our busy days of fitting it all in and ensuring students reach the demanding standards of our changing world, we might find ourselves focusing more on the skills needed to read and write rather than on the dispositions needed to sustain those practices. And while this might be effective in the short term, it fails to grow readers and writers who understand the power that literacy can have in their own lives over time. In a nutshell, we must make space in our lives, and in our classrooms, to do what readers and writers do.

Our Literate Hearts

While reading and writing may be intellectual activities, they are also callings from the heart. When we identify as readers and writers, it is typically not because we know *how* to read and write, but that we love to engage in reading and writing. We thread restorative literacy practices into our lives to bring intention and joy to our daily practices. But these restorative reading and writing practices might not always be evident in our classrooms.

If consistently tasked with reading and writing that feels like work—for example, by reading books of someone else's choosing and responding in artificial ways and by writing with little personal investment, with strict requirements and formats and for no audience other than the teacher—students may equate reading and writing with something to be completed rather than lived. We must offer plenty of opportunities to capture their reading hearts and writing spirits.

And the only way to accomplish that is to truly live as readers and writers ourselves, modeling our own authentic practices and inviting students to find their own joyful literate identities as well.

Our Literate Communities

Readers seek out other readers. Writers connect with other writers. Sharing our reading and writing lives honors our literate identities and invites us into a larger literate community. But it also does something more: it promotes accountability to our own literate lives. You see, being part of a thriving community where readers and writers regularly share books they are reading or written pieces they are working on often is inspiring. That participation fuels our reading and writing in ways that cannot be accomplished alone, supporting us to outgrow our current reading and writing lives and the way we see the world. Together, we can lift our level of reading and writing as we read and write within more-connected communities.

Our literate lives matter. Carefully tending to our habits and mindsets not only brings a sense of intentional well-being to our own literate lives, it sparks attention to how we are leading the way for our students to do the same.

Section 1

Reading

Preface to Section 1

When I look back at my history as a reader, I am drawn to the stories that taught me what reading is and why it matters in my life. While I don't have strong memories of being read to as a child, I do have vivid images of the books I was surrounded by. I've already mentioned one particularly powerful text in my early years: Jon Stone's *The Monster at the End of This Book*. I distinctly remember sitting with this book and being absolutely amazed that Grover was talking to me, inviting, even daring, me to join him in the pages of the book. For those that are not familiar with the book, it is told as a first-person narrative. Grover speaks directly to the reader, begging for help to avoid the monster and giving orders that readers ultimately disobey, much to his dismay. Early on, I learned that reading was a transaction, a lived experience with active participation and control over the fate of the story, a lesson that would impact the trajectory of my reading life. Armed with the expectation that reading would always be a highly experiential and personal act, I approached books as though they were pieces of my life, and devoured them throughout my childhood.

Today, as you might expect, I am an avid reader. I always have a book close by and my to-be-read stack (and Amazon cart!) is piled high with children's literature. Just as in my childhood, I am fiercely connected to the characters I meet and the places I travel through the pages of a book, often referring to them as if they were real. When my young daughter faced a difficult situation on the bus, I shared what Junie B. did during her difficult bus situation. When my son and I were driving through a particularly harsh storm, I compared our experience to Dexter's in Lauren Tarshis' *I Survived the Joplin Tornado.* When I needed a symbol to remind me of what I was capable of, I chose the octopus, just as Zoey did in Ann Braden's *The Benefits of Being an Octopus*. I connect with the characters and settings in books as though I have lived them myself, and cannot help but invite others into those worlds as well.

On one visit to a fifth-grade classroom, I shared the titles I was currently reading and asked students for suggestions for my next book. They eagerly shared titles, and we engaged in some spirited conversations about the books they were reading. Later that day, a student saw me walking down the hall with a Gordon Korman book sticking out of my purse. He ran up to me with a smile and said, "You really do read our books, don't you?" When I returned the next day, he shared one of his favorite books with me, as we were now connected through our bond as readers.

There is magic in connecting with students as fellow readers, magic that can only happen when teachers are readers themselves. When we lose sight of our reading lives and what real readers do, and add in the challenges of working with multiple instructional mandates, we can become susceptible to artificial practices that detract from our identities as readers: micromanaging text selection, maintaining unrealistic reading logs, requiring reading response that favors accountability over enjoyment, and forcing our own preferences as readers into our classrooms. These practices can chip away at students' identities as readers, creating unfortunate, but potentially lasting, impacts on students' ideas of what reading is and could be.

Now, I am not trying to give you the idea that simply picking up a book will turn your students into readers and remove the challenges you face as a literacy teacher that are beyond your control. What I *am* saying is that reconnecting with and reinvigorating your own reading life will remind you of the power it holds. You'll find a newfound dedication to your reading life that will spark reflection about your classroom practices. You might find practices that invite and inspire readers to celebrate, or you might find practices that you need to reassign value to or let go of to make room for more transformative and joyful reading experiences in your classroom. Either way, you're on the verge of a more robust reading life that will seep into the seams of your classroom.

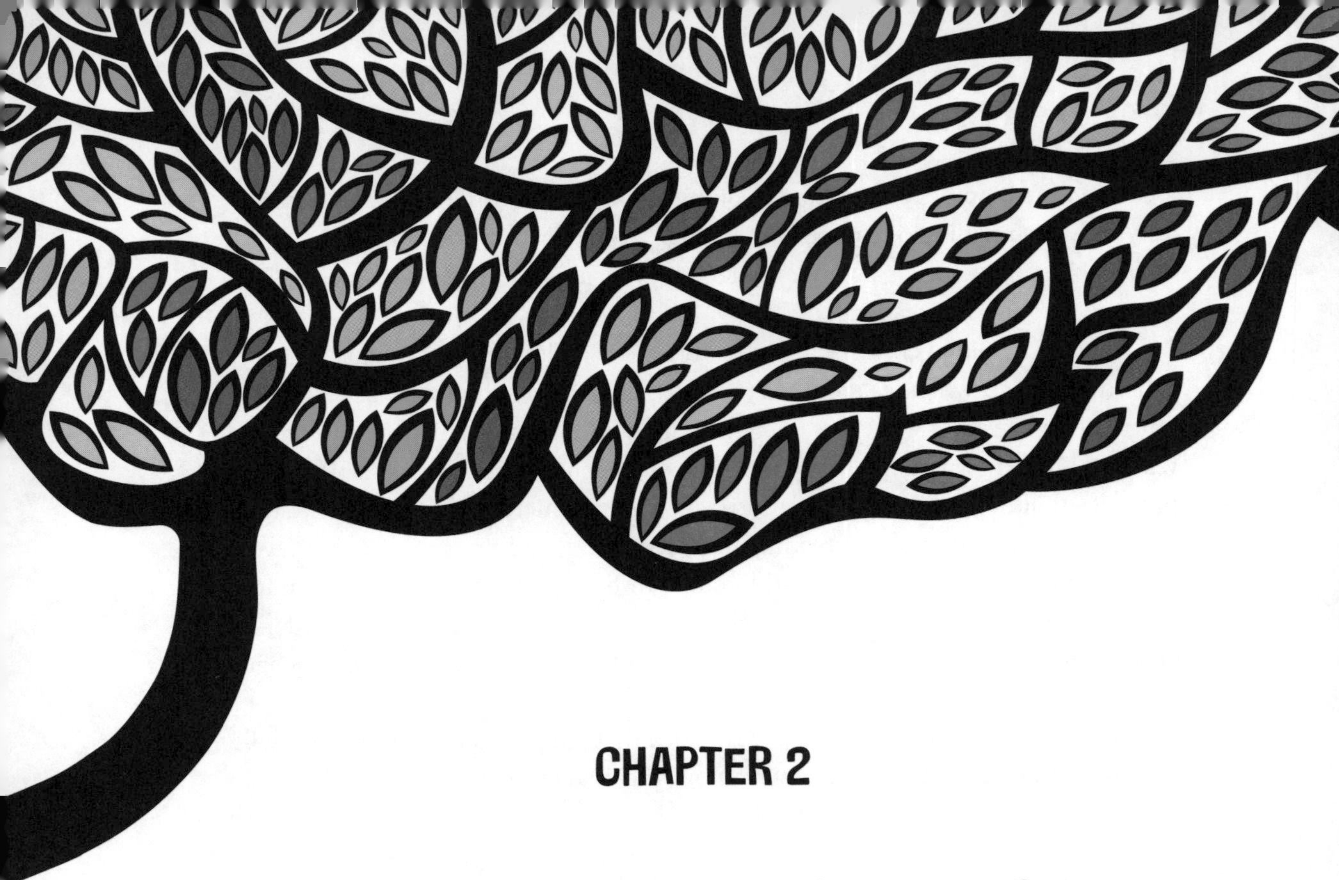

CHAPTER 2

Cultivate Our Reading Habits

I am a reader. I surround myself with books, make reading a priority throughout my day, and consciously develop reading habits that sustain my reading life. Let's begin with my favorite question to ask just about anyone I meet: "What have you been reading lately?" When asked, many teachers eagerly share their most recent titles with me. Others share a title that might be a bit dated and that they read a while back. And others might look at me sheepishly and mumble something about not having enough time to read the way they want to. I understand. Educators are incredibly busy and spend all of their time putting others' needs in front of their own, especially ones related to their reading lives.

Surround Yourself with Books

If I could give you only one idea to develop the habits that lead to a readerly life, it would be this: surround yourself with books. What better reminder to read than an actual book waiting patiently to be read! If we are going to cultivate our reading lives, we must surround ourselves with books: books we have read, books we are currently reading, and books we want to read next. But there's more. Simply having books is not enough—we need to strategically curate them and place them in locations where they will spur us to take reading action. Many of us have a space to collect books in our homes: bookshelves made especially for the task, a bedside table, or, in my house, the dining-room table that seems to be the catchall for everything. But while these locations might house our books effectively, they may not help us build consistent habits as readers. If the books are neatly tucked away, then our reading habits are neatly tucked away, too.

Build To-Be-Read Stacks

Book stacks are beautiful piles of books just waiting to be read. They take our lofty statements about the books we hope to read and turn them into concrete reminders to create the time to read them. Creating a book stack based on the reading life you envision for yourself is the first step in boosting your reading habits. Here's how:

First, spend some time exploring the books you truly want to read next. Browse through the recommended book lists online, read reviews on Goodreads, head to your local library or bookstore, or gain recommendations from friends, colleagues, and even your students. Think about the messages you want your stack to say about yourself as a reader. Does your stack reflect those choices? If not, keep searching for titles until you are content with the books in front of you.

Then, select three to five titles, purchase or borrow them, and physically stack them in a pile. It isn't enough to simply write down a list of to-be-read (TBR) titles. You must stack the actual books as a clear commitment to your reading life and a reminder to find the time to read them. Trust me. It works.

Place your TBR stack strategically in your daily line of vision. I prefer placing the books on my kitchen counter because I know I will see them each and every day, begging me to choose reading over the dishes. And it often works. Choose a place that will work for you. Perhaps it is the coffee table in your living room or your bedside table. Maybe it is right next to your favorite chair on the porch where the breeze comes in. Where you decide to place your stack is almost as important as the books that comprise it. By glancing at those books every day, you're more apt to find the time to read them. Scan the QR code to learn more about NCTE's Build Your Stack Initiative and grab some titles for your own!

https://bit.ly/3f4T29j

Scan for NCTE's #BuildYourStack

While I love a good book stack, there are only so many books that you can stack before they start to tilt and wobble. That's why I love creating book stacks with a few books for immediate reading and larger digital collections for long-term planning, and I encourage you to do the same. Here are a few options:

- Create a TBR stack in a photos app on your mobile device. First, create a new album and label it. Mine is simply called "Want to Read." Next, spend some time browsing your local library or bookstore, snap pictures of book covers that seem interesting, and add them to the album. I love taking pictures of the books friends and colleagues are reading, and I often ask them to get in the picture, too. That way, I can remember who recommended a particular book to me!
- Create a List on Amazon. I used to have a bad habit of adding to my Amazon cart all the books I was interested in buying "someday." After accidentally purchasing all the books in my cart, I started creating Amazon Lists instead. Lists are easy to make. Simply click on the "Add to List" button on the page for the book you are interested in. You can add the book to your public wish list or private shopping list, or you can create a personalized list instead.
- Create an account on Goodreads. Goodreads is a social platform that allows readers to connect with other readers and helps them decide what to read next. Creating a profile is quick and easy and adding books to your shelves is even easier. If you do not yet have a Goodreads account, go ahead and create one. If you do, spend ten minutes browsing the site and add a few books to your Want-to-Read bookshelf. If you want to maximize Goodreads, download the app to your phone so you can quickly and easily add books to your digital stack on the go.

Remember: it is one thing to create a collection and an entire other thing to actually use the collection to spark daily reading. While you might not physically see your digital stacks as you move about your day, challenge yourself to visit those spaces often. Move the app to the first home screen you see on your device for easy access and a reminder to open it.

Here's How to Bring It to the Classroom

Let's think about how we can bring book stacks through our own experiences to our classrooms. Invite your students to create their own book stacks so they always have a book at the ready. First, walk them through the process of how you created your own stack and why it matters for a robust reading life. Highlight each book you included and explain why. Then, give students time to gather three to five books that reflect the reading life they want to have and to showcase them prominently. Then, ask students, "If your book stack could talk, what would it say?" Students can write their messages on a speech-bubble template, attach it to their stack, and create reading goals based on their hope for their reading lives. You'll find examples in Figure 2.1.

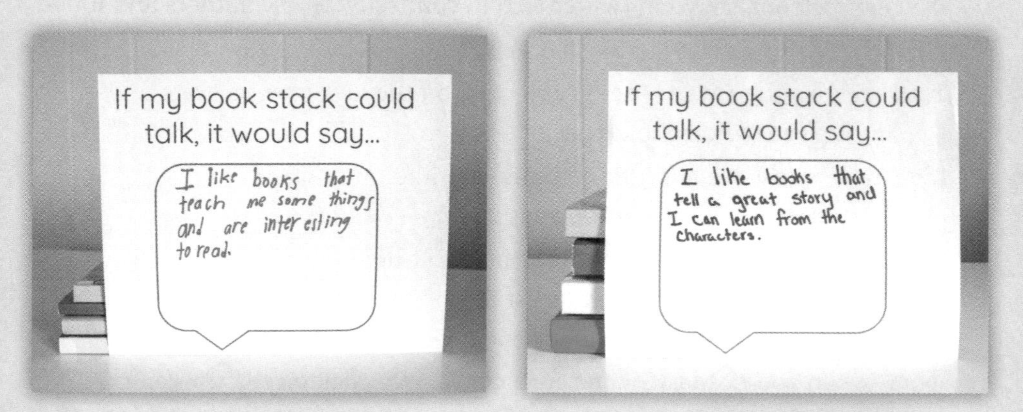

FIGURE 2.1 *Book stacks with speech bubble messages*

As readers continue to read and grow, you'll want to carve out time for students to replenish their stacks. Offer minilessons to help students choose good-fit books, explore new genres, and create stacks that represent the kind of readers they want to become. Give students opportunities to share their stacks with others and learn from their classmates' choices.

You might also create read-aloud stacks for your classroom. Bitsy Parks (2017) first introduced me to read-aloud stacks as a way to ensure that read-alouds stay part of the daily routine, are varied to meet students' interests, and spark students' curiosity. You can create a daily or weekly stack that reflects favorite authors, the content you are exploring, books newly added to the classroom library, mentor texts, and more. But don't stop at books alone; include poems, excerpts from larger books, and even articles to share with students. The stack of books patiently waiting will remind you and your students to make the time to read them.

Fill Your Social Media Feeds with Books

Social media has tremendous potential to boost our reading lives. I use it to boost my book knowledge by creating personalized lists of authors and illustrators and following hashtags dedicated to reading. Here, we'll explore how to use Twitter and Instagram to surround ourselves with books online.

You can personalize your Twitter feed to connect with the authors and illustrators you treasure most in three easy steps:

1. Head to your Twitter profile and click on the lists icon (it looks like a piece of notebook paper).
2. Create a new list and title it something like "Authors & Illustrators" or "Children's Literature."
3. Head to the profiles of your favorite publishers, authors, and illustrators. Add their feed to your list by clicking on the three dots and choose the "add to lists" option.

Now, when you head to Twitter, you can simply click on the list you created and instantly browse the feed of the authors you love. You'll find title ideas, sneak peeks of their new books, and even book giveaways!

Instagram has incredible potential to fuel our love of reading and children's literature. Start by following the Instagram accounts of children's book publishers and local bookstores. They post book recommendations, teasers for newly published books, and inspiration for continued reading. You'll find some of the publishers, authors, illustrators, and fellow booklovers I follow on Instagram in Figure 2.2.

While you may be tempted to stop with your favorite authors, challenge yourself to connect with authors and illustrators that are less familiar to you. Break down your reading walls and be open to new possibilities for yourself and your students.

Both Twitter and Instagram use hashtags to curate and organize information. By following a few hashtags dedicated to reading and connecting with books, you can scroll your way to a more robust reading life. Here are some of my favorite hashtags:

- #shelfietalk
- #titletalk
- #weneeddiversebooks
- #kidsneedbooks
- #booklove
- #ProjectLITchat
- #MGBookVillage

Instagram Account		Instagram Handle
Penguin Kids	→	@penguinkids
Holiday House Books	→	@holidayhousebks
Lee and Low Books	→	@leeandlow
Peter H. Reynolds	→	@peterhreynolds
Greg Pizzoli	→	@gregpizzoli
We Need Diverse Books	→	@weneeddiversebooks
Ruth Behar	→	@ruthbeharauthor
Kwame Alexander	→	@kwamealexander
Pernille Ripp	→	@pernillesripp
John Schu	→	@mrschureads

FIGURE 2.2 *Some of the publishers, authors, illustrators, and fellow booklovers I follow on Instagram*

Here's How to Bring It to the Classroom

Now, let's think about how we can connect our spirited scrolling on social media to the students in our classrooms. But before we get started, be sure to check your school's acceptable-use policy on social media and share your plans with your administrators.

Then, consider creating a class Twitter or Instagram account. Follow the authors and illustrators you are reading, and use your feed to spark interest and add books to your to-be-read stack. Project the feed on the Smart Board and browse with students if you can. Point out new book titles and posts from their favorite authors, and respond accordingly. If you're looking for some accounts to view for inspiration, follow Kathleen Sokolowski's third-grade class on Instagram, using @learningin215. Or, follow Jennifer Connolly's high-school English class on Twitter, using @ReadWarriors.

Post the books you are reading as a class. Upload the covers of the books you are reading, and tag the author, illustrator, and publisher, if possible. Add a comment or question and celebrate when your post earns a like or response. You can also ask for book recommendations for your class on either platform. Looking for your next read-aloud? Need a recommendation for a graphic novel in third grade? You might be surprised at the responses you receive from helpful educators and their students.

When used responsibly, the social technology connecting our world can connect our reading lives together and transform the culture of our classrooms, too. It makes sense to bring the technology of our world into the classroom, including social media, as long as it is done with care and attention to student privacy—and it abides by your school's policies.

Surround Yourself with Books

I love purses and bags. I still have my first book bag with my initials, which my father and stepmother gave me just before I started student teaching. My bag is my lifeline for what I hope to feel, do, and accomplish each day: books to be read, notebooks to be sketched and written in, colorful markers and sticky notes, a water bottle, and a snack (or two!). Each item acts as a trigger to ensure that I fill my time with practices that support my goals and renew my spirit. And now, it's time to design your own surroundings to support daily reading.

Grab the bag you carried with you today. It might be your school bag, your day bag, or even your purse. Dump out the contents onto a table, and inventory what you find. Yes, I said, "Dump out the contents onto a table." You need to physically see the contents to reflect on them. Pay attention to how you feel as you inventory your items, and think about the messages they might send you. Do the items reflect the kind of day you want to have? The kind of person you want to be?

Now, fill your bag to fuel your mind and spirit and set yourself up for reading success for the day ahead.

1. First, get rid of what you don't need and put any items aside that snuck their way into your bag but do not have a place there.
2. Then, arrange what you have left. Organize the papers that were simply stuffed in the bag. Gather the small items that fell to the bottom, and place them in a pencil case or zippered bag.
3. Add items that will remind you what matters most. First, add the book you hope to read during the day. Then, add other reminders, such as a water bottle and your notebook.

This might seem like a simple task to complete, but organizing the space around you facilitates the kind of life you want to live. And having your book within arm's reach at all times means you're ready to read if and when the opportunity presents itself.

Here's How to Bring It to the Classroom

We can surround our students with books by creating robust classroom libraries and lifelines to books. Access to books matters, and Scholastic (2018) provides clear guidelines for surrounding students with a broad range of high-quality texts. Each classroom library should boast a minimum of 750 books in good condition with a minimum of thirty books per student where the quality and content of the books are just as important as the quantity. Classroom libraries should include

- newly published books to capture students' attention and connect to the world today

- a rich variety of genres for all readers: realistic fiction, historical fiction, fantasy and science fiction, biography and autobiography, stories, classics, myths and legends, picture books, reference, poetry, comic books and graphic novels, and more
- books with characters and authors with a wide range of backgrounds and experiences so all students can see themselves within the pages of a book and learn more about the world around them
- a range of text complexity to ensure that all students have access to texts and topics they can successfully read and to topics and genres they choose.

https://bit.ly/3eQOlu9

Scan to learn more about It's All About the Books

We don't have to stop with our classroom libraries. Invite books to spill into other classroom spaces, and create book nooks that are sure to entice students to read. If you're interested in exploring how to boost your classroom library, scan the QR code to learn more about *It's All About the Books* (Mulligan and Landrigan 2018), a fantastic resource for building classroom libraries and book rooms.

Find Just Ten Minutes a Day

Years ago, I ended a mystery-reader session in a first-grade classroom by reminding students how important it was to find at least ten minutes a night to curl up with a good book. One little boy shot his hand in the air, waving for me to call on him. When I did, he blurted out as only a young, energetic child could: "Do you read ten minutes a night too, Mrs. A?" I stopped short because if I were honest, at that point of my life with three kids under three years old at home, I did not. Trying to hide my embarrassment, I told him that I tried to find those ten minutes just as he did and that sometimes it was easy and sometimes it was hard, but I would keep at it every day. Satisfied with the answer, he hopped off the carpet and went back to his seat. But that question haunted me. Here I was telling students to read every night and I could not hold myself to that same standard. Sure, I read for work and I read with children, but my personal reading life was sorely lacking. That moment with that young reader turned a page in my reading life, and I have worked ever since to maintain the kind of reading life that I can feel proud of in front of students. Now, the busyness of my life did not change. The dishes and laundry were still waiting for me, and my family did not lessen their busy schedule. Quite simply, I reprioritized reading in my life, and everything else fell into place. And by becoming a voracious reader myself, I better created a culture of literacy for the educators and students I worked with, something that must be lived, not only taught.

Give Habit Stacking a Try

We all engage in daily rituals and routines that determine the course of the day: how and when we wake up, get to work, fuel our bodies, keep the house clean, get our work done, take care of family members, head to bed, and many more. These habits are the unconscious tasks we engage in each day without fail and without thinking. But they are choices we've made—and those choices matter. They determine what we focus our time and energy on and how we feel as we proceed throughout our day. Since human beings tend to be creatures of habit, identifying those routines can work in our favor when attempting to grow our reading lives.

Let's begin by thinking about your daily habits. What are the things you do each day without fail? What are your morning routines? How do you get to work? What does your after-school routine look like? How about dinner or bedtime routines? Each of our routines gives our brain a signal to do something next. For example, when you get out of the shower, you might automatically brush your teeth. Or when you sit down at dinner, you might automatically say grace with your family. Or, when you walk into the house, you take off your shoes and place them on a shoe rack (how I wish my children had that habit firmly in place!). James Clear (2018) calls this idea "habit stacking," and we can use habit stacking to add a bit more reading to our lives as well. Here are a few ideas:

- After you turn on the coffee pot each morning, sneak in a few minutes of reading while the coffee brews (and then a few more taking those first heavenly sips).
- When you grab your lunch bag and head to lunch, grab the book you are reading, too.

- When you hop in the car to drive to school, listen to an audiobook to pass the time.
- When you grab the leash to walk the dog, open a podcast and listen to the latest book releases while you walk.
- When you sink down on the couch with your phone for some mindless scrolling, grab your book on the side table instead.

Think about your own routines and how you might pair one old habit with a new one. Try it for one week. If it doesn't feel right, then try a new one. But remember, it takes at least twenty-one days to make something a new habit, so keep at it over time and pick yourself back up if you fall off the wagon.

Here's How to Bring It to the Classroom

You can easily bring a new stacked routine to your classroom:

- Invite students to settle into the day with a good book. Add independent reading to their morning list of tasks and give students the gift of a soft start to the day.
- Add a read-aloud to snack time. Invite students to listen as they munch their snacks with classmates.
- Start independent reading time with a three-minute turn-and-talk to share reading selections with classmates.
- End the day with a book. Invite students to pack their bags for the ride home, grab their book, and settle in for five minutes of additional reading before leaving for the day.

These are just a few ideas, but get creative based on your own classroom schedule and routines, just as Leigh did. She paired her classroom restroom routines with an additional read-aloud—really! In her school, classrooms take scheduled breaks to the restroom after lunch. Often frustrated by students' extra-slow return from the restroom, she decided to read aloud in the hallway during this time. Not only did this build in extra time for reading, it encouraged students to return quickly to listen rather than dawdle.

Create a Reading Trip Wire

I first learned about the power of trip wires from Jan Burkins and Kim Yaris (2018). Trip wires are reminders we give ourselves to make positive changes in our practices. These small, yet tangible, visuals remind us to think, act, or feel differently based on the goals we have set for ourselves: the water bottle on my desk reminds me to drink it, the note on my fridge reminds me to choose a healthy snack, the quote written on a sticky note reminds me to think positively throughout the day. We can also create trip wires to remind ourselves to make time for what we value, in this case, independent reading.

Think about your personality, schedule, and daily routines. What kind of trip wire might work for you? Choose one of the following or invent your own:

- Books are great trip wires, as explored in an earlier invitation. Be sure to keep the book you are reading out and visible, not neatly tucked away in a bag or on a shelf.
- Set a reminder on your phone. If your goal is to read for a few minutes each night before bed, set a reminder on your phone to remind you to do just that.
- Personalize your coffee cup with one word: *Read.* This is a great, daily reminder of what you want to accomplish that day.
- Schedule it. Actually write it on your to-do list, or schedule it into your daily agenda. Don't leave reading for when your work is done. Make it a priority.
- Make use of sticky notes. Write reminders to read, and place them in compelling places: by the phone charger, on the television remote, or on your favorite reading chair.

Not all trip wires will have the same effect for everyone, so experiment and see what works for you.

Here's How to Bring It to the Classroom

We can easily create trip wires for our own students and fill our classrooms with reminders to read. Here are a few ideas:

- Create a screen saver on the classroom computer (and on students' computers, if possible) with a bold reminder to read.
- Write reminders to read on sticky notes, and place them around the room in unlikely spaces where students might find them.
- Create simple string bracelets for students to wear during the day. They can slip them on when they enter the classroom and then remove them at the end of the day. Or, they might slip them on before they leave for the day as a reminder to read at home that night.
- Add reminders to students' digital devices. You might post scheduled announcements on Google classroom or add daily events to their calendars.

Once you model how to create personalized reminders for reading in the classroom, you can make connections to students' home reading lives as well. Brainstorm personalized trip wires that students can use at home, and celebrate their success.

Use a Habit Tracker

I love journals. Typically I prefer writing and sketching on crisp, gleaming white pages, but there is something appealing about making lists and adding them to boxes to help keep my life aligned to what I value. Habit tracking describes the process of holding yourself accountable for certain habits you want to develop over time. A habit tracker provides a visual representation of your daily habits and offers a clear way to measure your progress, especially in your reading life. So, why not give one a try? The first step is to choose a habit tracker that is just right for you. Here are three options:

- Use your monthly calendar. In this method, you simply track the days you find time for reading on your current calendar. You might draw a green smiley face in each daily box, or you might add a pink dot to the corner instead. Regardless, mark the days you actually made time to read so they stand out.

- Use a one-page printable. Print a one-page habit-tracker template to chart your progress (see Figure 2.3). Place the habits you want to cultivate in the left column, and mark the squares in some way to celebrate your progress. You can download a PDF version of Figure 2.3 in the companion resources for this book: http://hein.pub/LeadingLiterateLives.

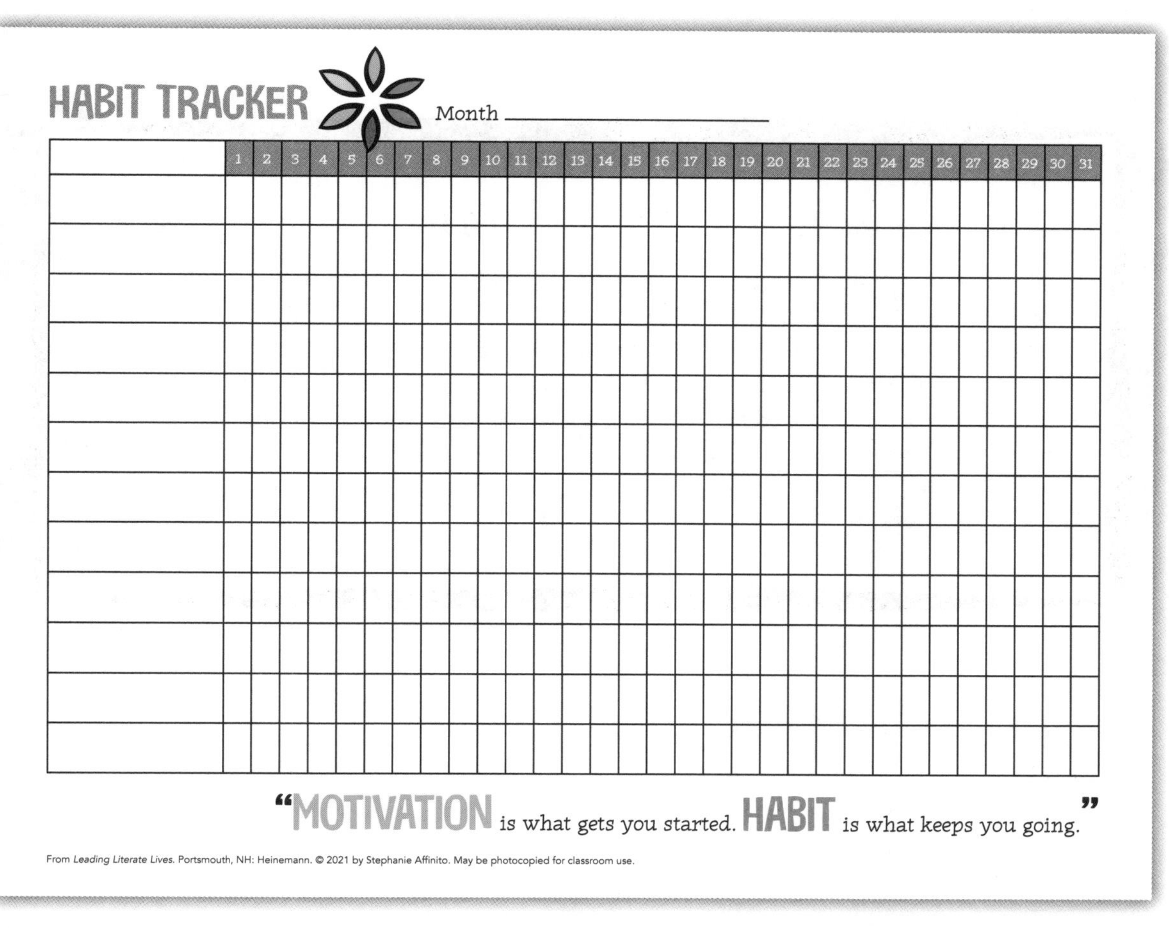

HABIT TRACKER

Month ____________________

	1	2	3	4	5	6	7	8	9	10	11	12	13	14	15	16	17	18	19	20	21	22	23	24	25	26	27	28	29	30	31

"MOTIVATION is what gets you started. HABIT is what keeps you going."

FIGURE 2.3 *A simple habit tracker*

- Go digital. There are multiple tools and apps to make habit tracking on a device quick and easy. You might try HabitBull, Productive, or Strides and explore which one looks and feels right to you. Users digitally track the days they engage in a new habit and track progress over time in much the same way they would use a printed tracker.

Now, you might think that you don't need a habit tracker—and you might not. But, you might be surprised at the accountability the simple act of shading in or digitally marking boxes provides to maintain your momentum. So, challenge yourself to use a tracker for a week—and then a month—and see how it supports your growing reading habits.

Here's How to Bring It to The Classroom

Your students can benefit from these same tools to maintain their own reading habits. You might start by printing out a simple calendar template for students to use each month. Each day they read, they mark the box in some way. Or, students can use the same tracker you use for your reading life. You could even create a kid-friendly page personalized to your students' grade level and personalities. Once you have introduced the idea of habit tracking to your students, be sure to carve out a minute or two each day to update the trackers and celebrate your students' reading progress!

Explore New Readerly Habits

I love the smell of books—the smell of a brand-new, haven't-cracked-the-spine-yet hardcover picture book, to be exact. When given a choice, I typically choose reading a physical book over a digital one. But technology is ever present in our lives today, including our reading lives. While some of those practices can hinder our reading lives (Did you know that if we replaced our daily social media scrolling with reading, we could read up to two hundred books per year?! [Chu

2017]), some of them can strengthen them. I've learned to appreciate the ease of digital texts, the mesmerizing world of audiobooks, and the ability of technology to instantly connect me to my next book. Perhaps you have already done the same, or perhaps you need a nudge to consider some new habits that can support your readerly life.

Learn to Love Audiobooks

The very first audiobook I ever listened to was *Lucky Broken Girl*. My daughter and I listened to Ruth Behar read as we drove to a softball tournament a few states away. We were mesmerized for the entire ride, and for the first time, felt that we arrived at our destination far too quickly as we wanted to finish listening. If listening to audiobooks is new for you, then definitely give this invitation a try.

Choose a book you want to read next and, instead of reading it traditionally, listen to it as an audiobook. You might choose to listen on Amazon Prime, Audiobooks, Audible, or an app from your local library. You might listen to the audiobook at home, on your commute, or as you multitask your way through house cleaning (my favorite!). Breathe deeply, listen to the words, visualize the text in your mind, and truly experience it. If possible, choose books narrated by the author to bring their words to life.

Once you have listened your way through the text, reflect: What were your impressions of audiobooks before giving this a try? Did they change? How was your experience listening to an audiobook different from traditional reading? Listening to an audiobook, especially one narrated by the author, can transform the reading experience. So, how might Audiobooks complement your current reading life and help you to build strong habits as a reader?

Here's How to Bring It to the Classroom

I have come to love audiobooks because of the experience they provide. While nothing can replace the way holding a book and turning the pages makes me feel as a reader, audiobooks make it so easy to immerse myself in the text. And what better way to build students' own love of reading than inviting them to do the same? Here are just a few ways to bring audiobooks into your classroom:

- When possible, give students the choice between reading a book or listening to it. Add a few audiobook apps to your class website for students to access. I like to use Epic, Vooks, and Hoopla. All students need is a pair of earphones to plug in and get hooked into a story.
- Refresh the listening station. Often abandoned as students head into the upper elementary grades, listening stations have a place in every classroom. Stock your station with beautiful picture books that can be listened to in a single sitting.
- Create your own audio files! You can create your own audio files for students to listen to, using a recording device and a QR code generator. Simply record yourself reading the book, article, or poem; upload it into Google Drive; and then link it to a QR code. Print the QR code, tape it into the book, and voilà—instant listening station. Just be sure to follow fair use guidelines. You'll find an example in Figure 2.4.

FIGURE 2.4 *Teacher-created QR code for listening station*

Push Play on Podcasts and Playlists

When I was young, I used to know almost every song on my favorite radio station, and I looked forward to getting in the car so I could sing along with my favorites. Now, as an adult, every time I get in my car, I press play on a podcast instead. Podcasts, episodes of audio files on a variety of topics, are the perfect way to connect you to your next book while you are driving to school or even folding the laundry.

You can find a podcast on almost any topic you choose, but I love listening to podcasts that book-talk books. Here are a few of my favorites:

- *Books Between*, created by Corrinna Allen
- *All the Books*, created by Book Riot
- *Scholastic Reads*, created by Scholastic, Inc.
- *What Should I Read Next?*, created by Anne Bogel
- *Levar Burton Reads*, created by LeVar Burton and Stitcher
- *All the Wonders*, created by All the Wonders
- *The Yarn*, created by Travis Jonker and Colby Sharp
- *Remember Reading?*, created by HarperCollins Publishers

This week, challenge yourself to listen to at least one episode of a podcast focused on books. Which will you try? When and where will you listen? Give an episode a try, but if you need something different (something shorter, longer, more upbeat, more focused, etc.), then explore the many podcasts available until you find one right for you!

Here's How to Bring It to the Classroom

Encourage your students to push "play" on podcasts, too. Here are a few podcasts focused specifically on reading and storytelling that they can explore:

- *Little Stories for Tiny People*, created by Rhea Pechter
- *Storynory*, created by Storynory
- *Book Club for Kids*, created by Kitty Felde
- *Circle Round*, created by WBUR
- *Fun Kids Book Club*, created by Fun Kids

You might play clips of podcasts and playlists at your morning meeting to jump-start conversation. Or, you might create a special podcast nook in your classroom as an additional literacy station for students to choose from. You might even link specific episodes to QR codes displayed in your library. And if you're hooked, students could even create their own!

Rely on Bots for What to Read Next

A bot is a software application that runs automated tasks over the Internet, and a social bot automatically fosters connections among users online. Think about your own Internet history. Have you ever searched for a particular topic on the Internet and then coincidentally found a related ad in your social media feed later that day? That is no coincidence—that is a social bot. And those same social bots can be used to broaden your reading life. Here are a few options for using them to your advantage:

- Head to an online bookseller, such as Amazon or Barnes & Noble. Type in a book that you recently read and enjoyed. Once you do, you'll find that the site automatically updates your feed to recommend other, similar books you might enjoy based on your search. Scroll through the titles, click on the ones that interest you most, and watch your recommended feed grow based on your additional interactions.
- Head to Goodreads. Goodreads is powered by voracious readers. So, when someone I am connected to in Goodreads recommends a book, I pay attention. And when the site recommends a book to me based on my bookshelves, I pay attention, too. If you click on a book in Goodreads, you'll find a "Readers Also Enjoyed" section on the right side of the page, toward the top. Scroll over the titles that interest you for an instant summary and reader ratings.
- Head to specially designed websites. There are multiple websites designed to connect you to your next book. Simply type in the

title you just finished reading or a book you enjoyed immensely. The website does the work and brings personally recommended titles to your screen. Try What Should I Read Next? (www.whatshouldireadnext.com), BookBrowse's "Read-Alikes" (www.bookbrowse.com/read-alikes), and/or Which Book (www.whichbook.net).

- Get personalized recommendations. This may be my dream job in another life: spending my days as a book matchmaker. There are services dedicated to learning about your reading interests in order to provide suitable book recommendations. Some local libraries offer this unique service through their websites. If your local library does not offer this service, head online and check out Readgeek (www.readgeek.com) and GoodReads' "Personalized Recommendations" (www.goodreads.com/blog/show/303-announcing-goodreads-personalized-recommendations) for personalized titles.

Here's How to Bring It to the Classroom

Technology has transformed our world in many ways, but the potential to use technology to spark connections between books and readers is incredibly exciting, especially when we use it to help students do the same. Some students will already know what bots are from their gaming adventures, but I've yet to meet a student that wasn't intrigued by the concept. Introduce the idea and invite students to use bots for book recommendations.

Start with the sites previously referenced for easy recommendations with no user name or account needed: What Should I Read Next?, BookBrowse's "Read-Alikes," and Which Book. But technology is not even needed to harness the appeal of a bot for book recommendations! Shelley, a literacy coach in upstate New York, used Google Slides to create bot-like book recommendations for her middle-school students to help them choose their next book and broaden their access to new titles. You'll find a poster similar to Shelley's in Figure 2.5.

Shelley considered the books popular with her students and created inviting posters showcasing related titles based on what her students enjoyed the most. She posted these displays around the school to infuse the building with books and to ignite students' passion for reading. You can, too!

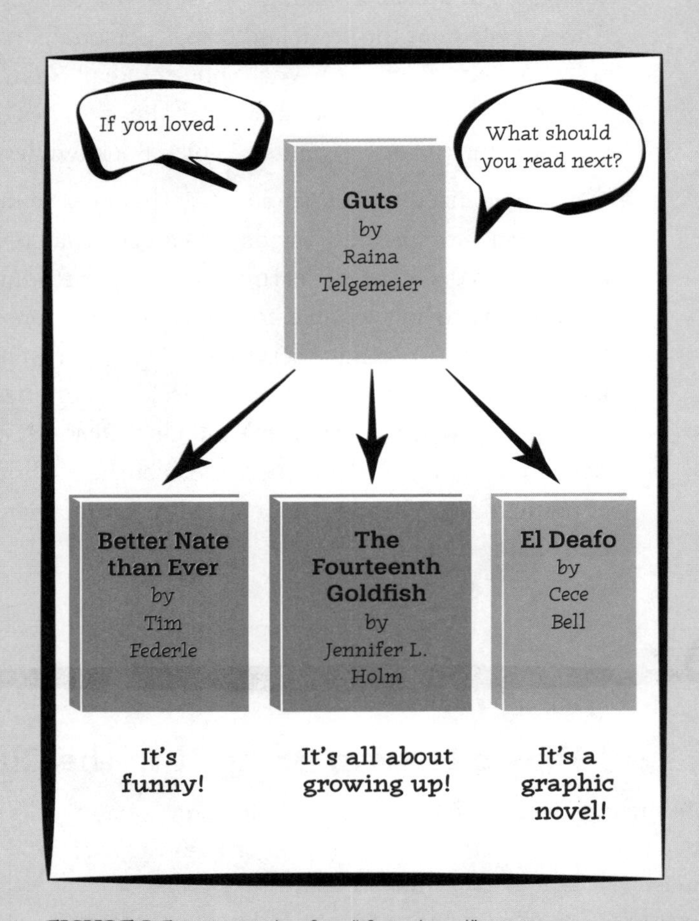

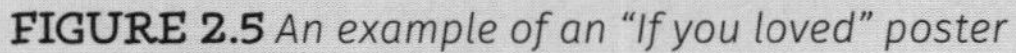

FIGURE 2.5 *An example of an "If you loved" poster*

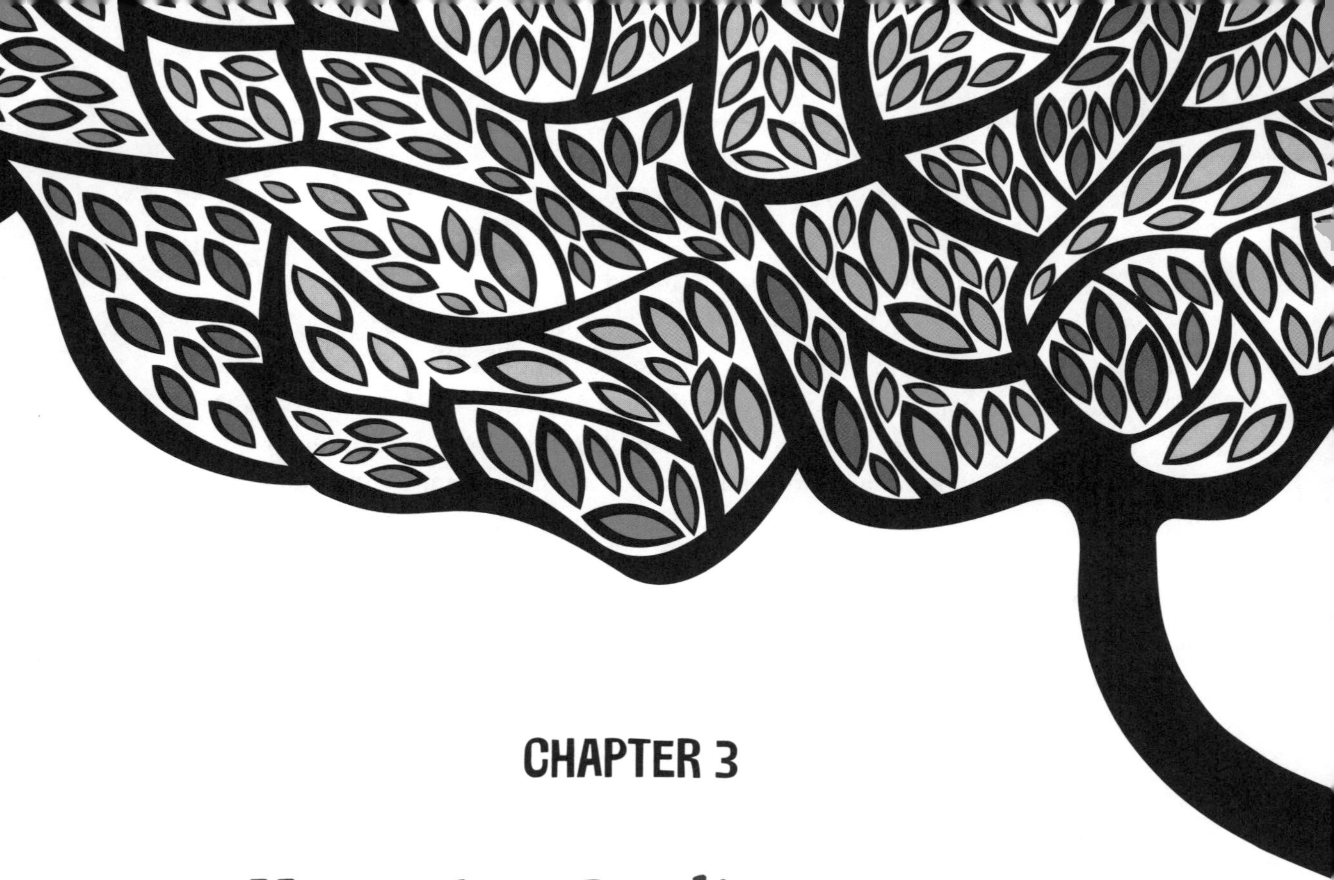

CHAPTER 3

Honor Our Reading Hearts

While reading may be an intellectual activity, it is a calling from the heart. When we identify as a reader, it is typically not because we know how to read, but because we love to read and we choose to engage as readers often, threading restorative reading practices throughout our days. Readers

- choose books based on their own personal reading interests, goals, and wishes
- live through the pages of books to meet new characters, to travel to new places, and to experience ideas impossible without reading
- respond to their reading in ways that are unique to each reading experience

- try new texts, genres, and ways of reading to broaden their reading life
- stretch outside their comfort zones to challenge their abilities and ideas of themselves and the world.

It is equally important, if not more so, to identify what readers do not do. Readers do not choose to read texts that are uninteresting or too difficult, or that they have no authentic purpose for reading. Readers do not engage in practices that diminish the value and joy of reading, such as proving their reading to others in artificial ways. Put simply, adults know themselves as readers and have the liberty of creating a reading life around their reading habits, practices, and identities.

We have a responsibility to tend to our own reading hearts so we can better care for our students. This means reading books that quench our adult curiosities and guilty pleasures, but it also means voraciously reading children's literature to better help our students do the same. I distinctly remember one weekend in New Jersey with my daughter. We were attending a softball tournament and enjoying some downtime in the sun, reading on lounge chairs by the pool. A fellow mom leaned over and asked, "Do you ever read adult books? I only see you with kids' books!" I smiled, explained why, and admitted that I often enjoyed children's literature even more as it consistently gave me a new perspective for looking at the world through children's eyes.

We must read current books written for today's students. Knowing these titles helps us better connect with our students and live in their world. We must read across genres and make a conscious effort to read books that our students enjoy, even if they are not our own preferred genres. We must read a diverse selection of books. We cannot solely read books that mirror our own lives; we must read books that offer us a window into new characters, perspectives, and ideas. We must mind our reading gaps and read books we might not choose initially to be sure we do not pass those gaps along to our students. The bottom line? Our reading hearts matter. They are literally the heartbeat of our reading lives, the reason we read in the first place: to be changed through our reading experiences. And those hearts must be cared for, nurtured, and protected so we can give the same gift to our students. If we truly live as readers ourselves, we are more likely both to invite students to find their own joyful reading identities and to privilege practices in our classrooms that cultivate them.

Embrace Your Reading Identity

While my favorite genre to read is realistic fiction, I also have a penchant for books focused on self-improvement: how to be happier and more successful, how to finally learn to cook (someday!), how to take control over my finances and, more recently, how to embrace a more authentic life. As I devoured this genre, I happened to hear motivational speaker Jim Rohn's statement that we are the average of the five people we spend the most time with. Ponder that for a moment. Who are the five people you choose to (or must) spend the most time with? How do those five people shape your daily thinking and actions?

Similar questions can apply to our reading lives as well. What are the last five books you have read? When were the last five times you found time to read? Who were the last five people you chose to discuss your reading with? What do your responses say about who you are as a reader? This set of questions will guide your exploration of your reading identify.

Honor Your Reading Preferences

We all have unique reading practices that appeal to our own needs and preferences as readers: where and when we prefer to read, the texts we choose to read, how we read and engage with those texts, who we choose to share our reading with, and more. Turn to a fresh page in your notebook and complete the following sentence stems without hesitation or censoring:

- I am a reader because . . .
- I am the kind of reader who . . .
- As a reader, I choose not to . . .
- I want to be the kind of reader who . . .

Look back over your notebook page and take a minute to reflect on what you have written. Does the kind of reading life you currently have reflect the kind of reading life you truly want? If it does, celebrate! If it doesn't, don't worry. Look at your notebook page and choose one aspect of your reading life you'd like to indulge without abandon or guilt. Do you want to read the gossip magazines while curled up in your favorite chair? Go for it. Do you want to read an adult graphic novel outside by your favorite tree? Or, do you want to read a self-help book on how to conquer your fears while enjoying a latte? Do that too. Our reading preferences are unique expressions of who we are as readers, and we all deserve to engage in reading for the sheer pleasure of it. So, indulge yourself and see how it makes you feel as a reader.

Here's How to Bring It to the Classroom

How do your own preferences as a reader seep into your classroom? Some of us might prefer silence while reading and, therefore, require silence while reading in our classrooms. Some of us might prefer to read at our desks so we can easily write in our notebooks and, as a result, require our students to do the same. We all have certain reading habits and practices we need to be successful. And those habits and practices are unique to each of us. What works for one reader might not work for another. But as the lead reader in our classroom, we might inadvertently require students to adopt our own reading preferences simply because they work for us. Here's how to avoid that:

- Learn about your students' identities as readers. You might ask them to draw a reader just as you did in the beginning of this journey, or you might have a heartfelt conversation with them about their beliefs about reading.
- Survey their preferences and practices. Ask students about where, when, and how they like to read.
- Offer students choice in the ways they read books, how they respond to their reading, and how they share their reading with others.
- Carve out spaces in your classroom to meet your students' varied needs and honor their preferences as readers. You might create a quiet zone for readers who prefer to read in silence or comfortable spaces throughout the classroom for those students who like to curl up with a book instead of at their desks.

Read to Explore Your Sense of Self

Reading is an exploration. With each book we open and each page we turn, we learn about ourselves and the way we operate in the world. The identities we carry in the world have a tremendous impact on our reading lives, and consciously choosing books related to them can connect us even more to our reading hearts.

I first learned this activity from Laura Sackton (2017), a Book Riot blogger, and have modified it to make it my own. Turn to a new page in your notebook and list the identities that are important to you: wife, father, teacher, crafter, cook, runner, and more. Strive for at least five identities that showcase who you are and how you experience your world. Examine your list and choose three that are central to who you are and that matter most to your well-being.

Then, choose three books that explore those three important identities in some fashion. You might choose a fiction book focused on strong family bonds or a nonfiction book about gardening. Or, you might choose a book with a character who travels the world, matching your own desire. Spend some time researching new books and write a few possible titles next to your listed identities.

Next, choose three identities that do *not* hold true and explore books that embody those identities as well. List them on the page. By doing so, you'll gain insight and empathy for other ways of living and being in the world. You'll find my completed identity book list in Figure 3.1 as an example to use for your own.

Use this newly created list to choose books to add to your TBR stack, and pay careful attention to your responses to the books. How are they validating who you are? How are they helping you reach for new ideas and perspectives? But here's one more thing to consider: your identities shift and change over time and, therefore, so does the timeliness of the books you choose to read. What might not be a good fit for you right now might be later on. And what works perfectly for your reading life today could be completely wrong for you in ten years. With each passing day and with each passing page, we change. So, too, should our reading lives.

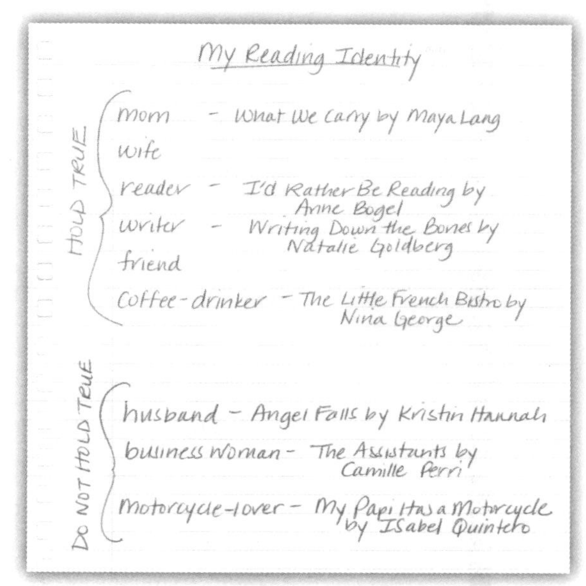

FIGURE 3.1 *My list of reading identities*

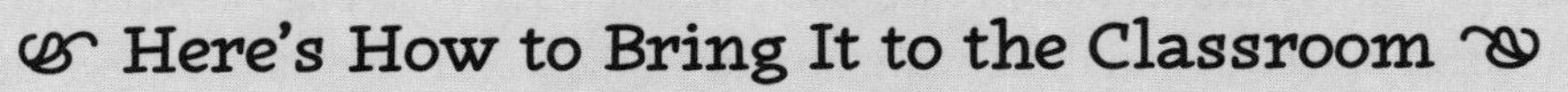

Here's How to Bring It to the Classroom

All readers have a right to read books that help them explore their reading identities and discover their sense of self through personally meaningful reading experiences. Therefore, our classroom libraries should be inclusive: filled with books that respect the uniqueness of each and every student.

Tricia Ebarvia (2017) defines *inclusive practices* as "those that guarantee the perspectives and contributions of all people—especially of diverse backgrounds who have been traditionally marginalized such as LGBTQ+ individuals, people with disabilities, and people of color—are given equal recognition, attention, and care in all learning environments." The texts we provide students access to have the potential to shape their views of themselves and of the world and must be examined carefully. While there are checklists and tools to help you evaluate your libraries for diversity and inclusivity, the best way to take stock of how well your classroom library reflects your students is to involve the students themselves in the evaluation.

Follow Jess Lifshitz's (2016) lead and invite students to audit your classroom library together. Have them randomly choose a number of books for your classroom library (this number will depend on the age of the students and the space you have for this work), examine the cover, and read the book summary, if provided. Have students note their thinking on a simple chart as they skim the pages of each book and consider questions like these:

- Who is the author and illustrator? Do they look like me?
- Who are the characters? Do they look like me?
- What is the genre of the book? Do I like reading in this genre?
- What does the story seem mostly about? Am I interested in this kind of story?
- What setting does the story take place in? Is it like my community?
- What challenges are the characters facing? Are they challenges I am facing, too?
- What facts might I learn from this book? Am I interested in this topic?

https://bit.ly/3naGIXM

Scan to learn more about Jess Lifshitz's classroom library analysis

These questions can start important conversations, and older students can certainly dig deeper into their analysis as Jess Lifshitz's fifth graders did. Scan the QR code to read the original blog series about the project.

Ask students about their wishes for the classroom library to learn more about their hopes for reading and to better support your library efforts. In her 2017 blog, Jennifer Williams suggests asking the following:

1. What types of characters would you like to see represented in our books?
2. What challenges does our community face that should be reflected in our classroom library?
3. What is one thing people do not know about you that you wish they did?
4. Complete this sentence: I want to read a story about someone who ______________________________.

Lead a conversation around these questions, ask students to privately reflect through writing, or get more creative and create a reading confessional inspired by Scholastic's Alycia Zimmerman (2018). All you need is a quiet corner of the library and a mobile recording device, such as an iPad or Chromebook. One by one, students video record confessions of their reading lives and wishes they have for their classroom. Simple to implement, this practice can empower students' voices in shaping their classroom libraries and even help teachers outgrow literacy practices that aren't serving them well.

Wondering where to find diverse titles? Head to We Need Diverse Books (https://diversebooks.org) and start exploring. I highly recommend their *Our Story* app, a tool that links readers to titles with diverse content and written by authors from marginalized communities. Teachers and students complete an interactive quiz to discover the perfect book to stretch their reading life. While bringing diverse books into our classroom libraries is a start, it isn't enough; we must also read them, discuss them, grapple with them, learn from them, and embody the lessons they teach. If this is new territory for you, spend some time learning how to explore diverse texts and topics with your students. I recommend that you start with #DisruptTexts and follow Tricia Ebarvia, Lorena Germán, Kimberly Parker, and Julia Torres on social media.

Shelley Fenton and Krista Senatore, two literacy coaches from upstate New York, created the Classroom Library Project as a way to transform classroom libraries by abandoning levels and bringing in new, diverse selections to inspire readers. They remodeled multiple classroom libraries into inviting, engaging spaces with books that reflected the students' identities and interests. Together with students, they weeded books, remodeled spaces, reorganized shelves, and brought in new books to connect with readers. To learn more about their classroom library project, visit Shelley and Krista's blog. Open your Internet web search and type in "Lit Coach Connection." Once you're on the home page, search for "classroom library project."

Inspire Reading with Personal Goals

As proficient readers, we typically do not set explicit goals for our reading life. Chances are we consistently read books of our own choosing that are at an independent reading level written on topics that we enjoy and want to read about in a space that is suitable to our reading preferences. We adult readers typically read books because we want to read them, not because we want to explicitly deepen our reading prowess. Yet, choosing personally meaningful goals can bring renewed energy to our reading lives.

Perhaps you want to slow your reading pace to ensure you deeply understand your reading. Maybe you want to develop your background knowledge to tackle a historical fiction book you've been wanting to read. Maybe you want to cultivate your reading notebook entries to better remember the books you plan to read later on. Now is your chance to inspire your reading life with personal reading goals. You'll find three possible goals with ideas for how you might achieve them in Figure 3.2.

Reading Goal	Reading Actions
Slow my reading pace to deeply connect with the storyline in a book.	• Create uninterrupted time for reading to ensure I am not rushing through the text because of time restraints. • Identify stopping points as I read to reflect on the events unfolding. • Build a habit of relating the text back to my own life and thinking about the lessons I am learning.
Increase my background knowledge on a topic to better understand historical fiction.	• Google the historical time period to gain background knowledge. • Watch brief video clips of the era to better visualize the setting of the book. • Keep track of my questions and confusions on sticky notes as I read, and seek answers and clarifications.
Track my thinking in a reader's notebook.	• Pair my notebook with my current book so it is always on hand. • Jot and sketch as I read. • Share my notebook with fellow readers as an impetus to keep it up to date.

FIGURE 3.2 *Possible reading goals and ways to achieve them*

So, what goals might you set to inspire your reading life? Brainstorm a few in your notebook. Be sure to choose goals that you really want to work on, not goals you *think* you should work on. These should be meaningful, authentic, and personal goals that you'll look forward to reaching. Now, choose one goal, and brainstorm at least three reading actions that could help you meet it, as I did. Spend some time over the next week making a conscious effort to attempt all three readerly actions related to your goal. Keep track of your goals, your actions, and your thinking in your notebook to archive your reading life and, later, to provide powerful models for your students to do the same.

Here's How to Bring It to the Classroom

Chances are you have reading goals for each of your students focused on the curriculum, the standards, or school literacy initiatives. Think about who owns those reading goals. Did you create them *for* your students? Or *with* your students? Or did they create their own? While our teaching must have a central goal aligned to the standards and curriculum, our reading goals should be personal expressions of what we *want* to work on as readers as well as what we *need* to work on. If you do not have students set personalized goals, start by learning more about what this could look like. I recommend using Jennifer Serravallo's (2015) *The Reading Strategies Book* as a starting point.

If you already have reading goals for each of your students, consider who created them. If you created them based on assessment data alone, try creating them together with your students instead to ensure they focus on students' reading hearts as well as their minds. If you already cocreate reading goals with your students, consider handing over even more independence. Provide minilessons on how readers create personalized goals, and help students create anchor charts of possible goals and ways to meet them. And most importantly, work with students to revise those goals throughout the year. While you might choose an overarching goal for a student over a longer period of time, helping them break down those goals into weekly or monthly strategies gives them a sense of ownership over their own reading life, something every reader deserves.

Find Passion and Purpose in Reading

Pull the cover back on your true inner reader and think about the reading that sets your heart on fire. What is your real purpose? Is it to meet new characters and learn from the events in their lives? Is it to escape your own? Is it to learn something new to quench your curiosity or better your life in some way? Is it to learn from the past to better impact the future? Is it to simply savor the power of words and playfully bring them into your lives? Voracious readers read with passion and purpose, devouring books to change who they are, what they feel, and how they act in the world with each turn of the page. Without passion and purpose, reading simply becomes something to do, something to pass the time, and something that can get pushed aside for more pressing tasks or a different pastime. But if we bring passion and purpose into our reading lives, reading becomes a way of living in the world, seeing it with new eyes, and, possibly changing the trajectory of our lives.

Read with an Open Heart

While many of us might curl up with a good book to relax and even drift off to sleep in the evening, to truly experience reading as a transformative practice, we must read wide awake: read with open eyes, minds, and hearts to see the world in a new and different way. Amy Krouse Rosenthal (2013) reminds her readers to pay attention: "For anyone trying to discern what to do w/their life: pay attention to what you pay attention to. That's pretty much all the info u need." This same principle can apply to our reading lives as well: here are three powerful ways for you (and your students!) to pay attention and read wide awake with an open heart:

- Take a character x-ray. Character x-rays, inspired by Jewett (2011) and Short (2008), are exactly what they sound like: x-rays of a character that help us see characters for their inner values and beliefs, rather than only for their surface characteristics. Turn to a clean page in your notebook and choose a character from the current book you are reading. Draw the outline of a body and add a heart to the middle. On the outside of the body, list the character's physical characteristics. On the inside, list the traits, values, and beliefs your character embodies. How does this help you think more deeply about the character and the text in general? Add to your x-ray over time to pay close attention to how the character changes over the course of the book and be open to the lessons you might learn as a result.

- Try a RAN chart. A Reading and Analyzing Nonfiction (RAN) chart is a newly imagined KWL chart. Created by Tony Stead (2004), the chart helps readers to read and analyze nonfiction text with an open and engaged mind. Draw a table in your notebook and label the columns like those in Figure 3.3.

What I Think I Know	Yes! I was Right!	I Changed My Mind!	New Information I Learned	Things I Still Wonder About

FIGURE 3.3 *A blank RAN chart*

Before reading your next nonfiction selection, go ahead and give this a try. Jot down all the information you know (or think you know) about the topic. As you read, pay close attention to what you learn to confirm or disconfirm your prior knowledge, and mark the appropriate column. After reading, jot down a few new facts you learned and end by noting the things you still wonder about to help drive you into your next book. Add to your chart over time to represent your changing thinking about the world around you.

- Create a collection of quotes in your notebook. Each time you come across a quote that speaks to you in some way, write it down, word for word, and note the title and author of the book it was in. Here are a few of my favorites:
  - "You have to be taught to be second class; you're not born that way." (*The Legendary Miss Lena Horn* by Carole Boston Weatherford)

- "Hollows are proof that something bad can become something good with enough time and care and hope." (*Wishtree* by Katherine Applegate)
- "Great minds don't think alike." (*Fish in a Tree* by Lynda Mullaly Hunt)
- "How will the world change if we do not question it?" (*The Magician's Elephant* by Kate DiCamillo)
- "Sometimes when you're surrounded by dirt, you're a better witness for what's beautiful." (*Last Stop on Market Street* by Matt de la Peña)

My pages of quotes vary. Some are plainly written in ink. Others are surrounded by swirls of color and shapes. I also have a digital quote collection in a photo album on my phone. I snap pictures of compelling pages as I read and save them for later reflection, often adding them to my notebook. You should, too.

Here's How to Bring It to the Classroom

As adult readers, we make decisions about our reading lives that impact the way we think and feel about reading and the way we think about the world. But, in many schools and for many students, reading is seen as a mandate, not an invitation. Students' wide-awake reading is often managed both in school and at home: required texts, forced reading logs, mandated reading responses, artificial quizzes, and more. These artificial practices hold students accountable for their reading rather than celebrate it. So, what steps can we take to change that?

Gather a few samples from your students' reading responses, and mine them for signs of their reading hearts. Do they offer a glimpse into students' thoughts, reactions, and questions as they read? Do they provide spaces for students to share the connections and disconnections they are making? Do they offer students opportunities to think forward about the text rather than only responding back? Or, do they mainly require students to prove their reading in an academic way—for example, by discussing the theme of the text without actually personalizing it to their own lives, by analyzing character traits without connecting to themselves, or by answering literal comprehension questions that do not take into account students' own thinking? Your insights will uncover the messages your curriculum might be sending to students and prompt you to make changes to better focus on your students' reading hearts as well as on their cognitive skills. Look ahead in your curriculum and notice when students have the opportunity to strengthen their reading skills versus their reading identities. How balanced is that ratio? Make sure students have at least one opportunity to better connect with their reading hearts in the next unit of study.

You might introduce your students to the three ways you just explored to read wide awake: character x-rays, RAN charts, or quote collections. Make it very clear that the sole purpose of reading is to be impacted by the text in some way and the only way to do that is to read with an open heart.

Make Room to React to Texts

Books have the potential to change who we are as readers and as people; they provide lessons that can be quickly forgotten if not captured. Have you ever read a powerful book only to struggle to remember the details later on when recommending it to a friend? I know I have. Capturing our reactions to texts ensures they become part of who we are as readers.

I invite you to create a new section in your notebook: a space to react to your reading. Turn to a clean page and add the date and the title of your current book. Then, react as you read. There are no rules to reacting to a text. Anything goes. The idea is to simply react to your reading in whatever way feels right based on the interaction you are having with the text before, during, or after reading. You might

- keep track of the characters you meet or create a simple timeline of the major events to help keep your reading focused
- sketch or draw an important scene to keep it fresh in your mind
- note the connections you make to the book: connections to yourself, to other texts, and to the world
- create a list of new facts that you do not want to forget

- collect quotes that made you stop and think because they were so powerful
- ask questions of the book, the author, the characters, yourself, and the world
- draw or sketchnote your thinking, using color, icons, and frames to capture your understandings.

Explore different ways to make your thinking visible and see what works for you. Experiment with colored pens, pencils, and markers to capture your mood as well as your message. Now, some readers prefer to do this kind of thinking on sticky notes instead so they can easily be placed in the book as visible tracks of reading. I do this, too. Then, once the book is finished, I gather the sticky notes together and tuck them into my reader's notebook for safekeeping.

Here's How to Bring It to the Classroom

As you experimented with ways to react to the texts you were reading, you were in full control over when, how, and why you responded to the text, a luxury our students do not often share during the school day. They are often told when to respond, how to respond, and even what to respond about. But, hopefully, taking time to react to your own texts as a reader showcased just how important it is to have a space to react in a way that makes sense with that book at that time.

So, what could you do to help your students have a similar experience? Start by trying a new form of reading response in your classroom. Which options listed on pages 49–50 worked best for you as a reader? Which hadn't you tried before that supported your thinking? Share your thinking, and your notebook with students as a model for their own, and make sure they have spaces to do the same. Krista Senatore, a literacy specialist in upstate New York, keeps a reading sketchbook where she sketches her responses to each book she reads as a model for her students. She uses her notebook in minilessons and conferences as a way to introduce students to their possible next book to read. You'll find a picture of one of her pages in Figure 3.4.

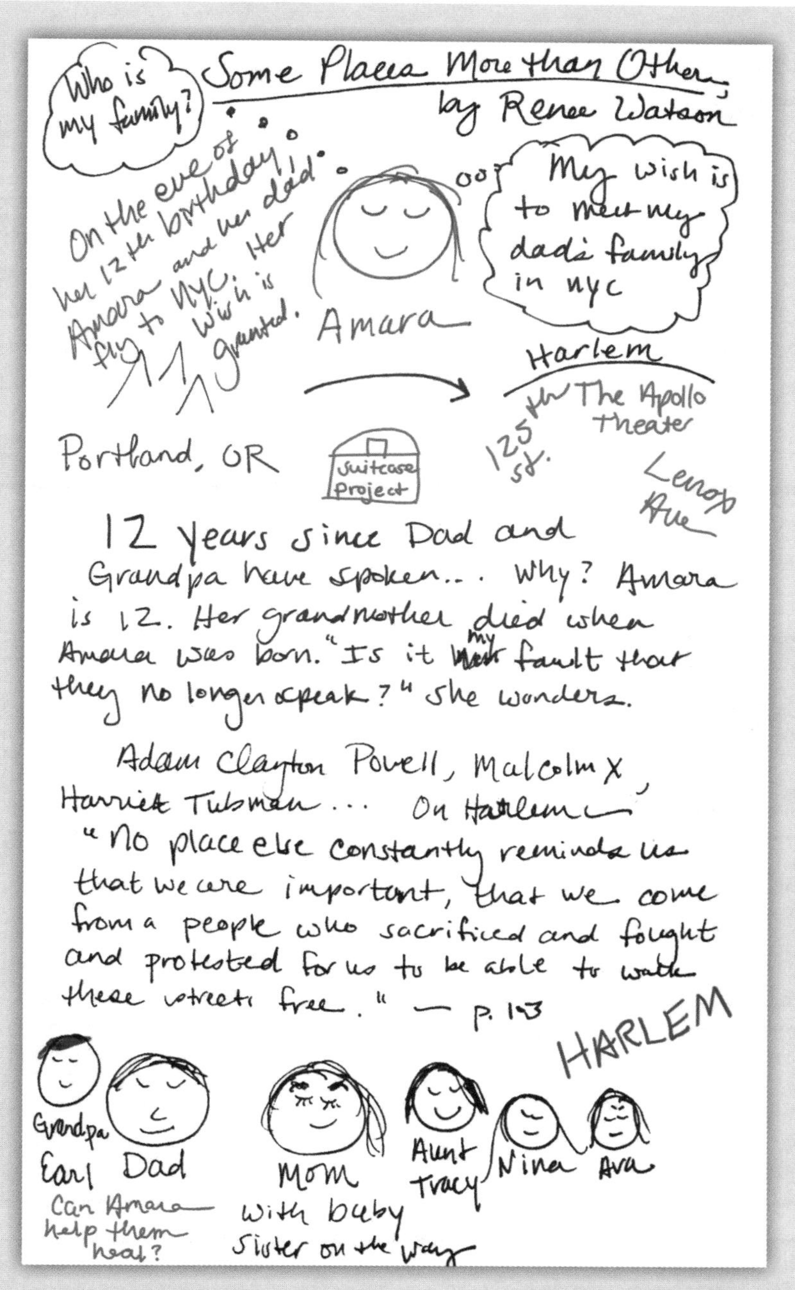

FIGURE 3.4 *A page from Krista Senatore's reading sketchbook for students*

You might also create choice boards that provide multiple options for students to make their reactions to their texts visible, letting them choose how and when they will respond to books based on how they were impacted as readers. An example of a reading-response choice board can be found in Figure 3.5.

The good news? We have control over how reading is perceived in our classrooms. If we consistently require artificial responses to reading, then reading will become artificial to our students. But if we offer multiple ways to react to text that support students' individual responses and cater to their preferences for recording them, then reading will become something that impacts who they are. We may not be able to control the standards, curriculum, or assessments, but we can effect small changes that will make all the difference in the world to students' reading hearts.

Reading-Response Choice Board

Choose how to respond to your book based on your own personal reactions as you read:

Create a list of your favorite quotes from the book.	Write an email to the character. What would you say to him or her?	Choose your favorite scene. Sketch it and describe how it makes you feel.
Create a character x-ray. What does your character show on the outside? What is he/she like on the inside?	Create a timeline of important events.	Create a list of connections and disconnections you had while reading.
Write a summary of the book so you can share it with a classmate.	Rewrite a part of the story you wished went differently.	Create a digital poster to represent your reaction to the book.

FIGURE 3.5 *A reading-response choice board*

Live Curiously Through Books

Merriam-Webster (2020c) defines *curiosity* as the "desire to know: interest leading to inquiry." Curious people wonder and question, inquire and investigate.

Curious readers read with an open mind, seeking to learn by actively engaging as they read, often harnessing the power of technology in the process. When my son and I were reading *I Survived the Joplin Tornado* by Lauren Tarshis, we read with a device close by. Why? We looked up what a Navy Seal trident insignia actually looked like. We used Google Earth to look up Joplin, Missouri. We watched the original news briefs of the tornado, just as the main character in the story did. We read about tornado weather pods to better understand how they work and potentially save lives. We viewed real images of the destruction to more fully experience the harrowing events the characters endured. We lived curiously through the pages of a book and deepened our reading experience together in a way that could not be achieved without these practices. Living curiously through books enriches the reading experience. So, how might you live curiously through the books you are reading?

- Find the setting of the book you are reading on Google Maps. Explore the area to get a firsthand idea of what the setting might actually look like—and add the location to your bucket list of places to visit.
- Search for images to help you visualize objects and items from the book. My favorite find? Seeing the same brilliant blue from the lapis lazuli stone that Beverly Tipinksky saw on the cover of a book in *Beverly, Right Now* by Kate DiCamillo.
- Look up vocabulary in a digital dictionary to broaden your language and vocabulary. Did you know that *sunder* means "to break apart or separate"? I do now.
- Explore new concepts and ideas. Watch videos, read online articles, and learn from supplemental resources. YouTube, Great Big Story, and The Kid Should See This are great places to start.

Living your way through books curiously invites you to experience them firsthand, actively learning about the world without ever leaving your home. So, grab a device and give it a try the next time you read a book—and see where it takes you. Then, share the experience with your students.

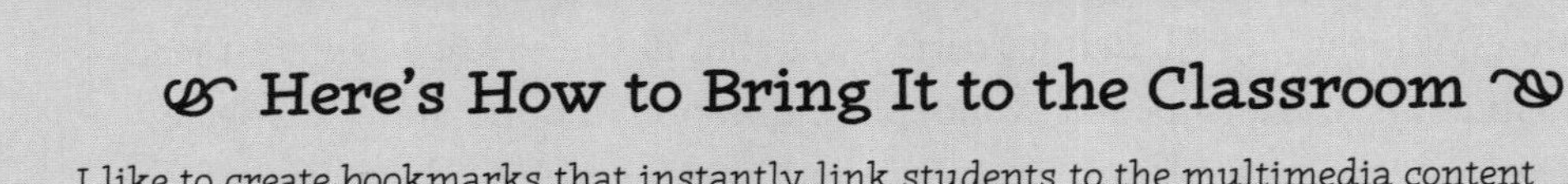

Here's How to Bring It to the Classroom

I like to create bookmarks that instantly link students to the multimedia content explored on page 53. You'll find an example of a bookmark I created for an I Survived book in Figure 3.6.

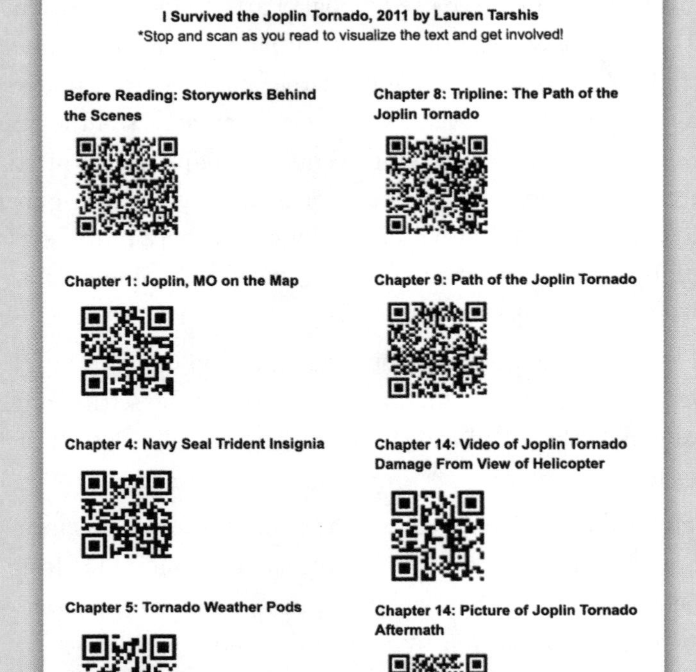

I Survived the Joplin Tornado, 2011 by Lauren Tarshis
*Stop and scan as you read to visualize the text and get involved!

Before Reading: Storyworks Behind the Scenes

Chapter 1: Joplin, MO on the Map

Chapter 4: Navy Seal Trident Insignia

Chapter 5: Tornado Weather Pods

Chapter 8: Tripline: The Path of the Joplin Tornado

Chapter 9: Path of the Joplin Tornado

Chapter 14: Video of Joplin Tornado Damage From View of Helicopter

Chapter 14: Picture of Joplin Tornado Aftermath

FIGURE 3.6 *A QR code bookmark for students reading* I Survived the Joplin Tornado

Here are the steps to create your own bookmarks for students:

1. Create a bookmark template. I simply divide a document into two columns to create oversized bookmarks, but you may want to get more creative. Label each side with a section of the book: one for each chapter or one for each block of text students will read.

2. Read the chapter/section. As you read, think about the content that could deepen students' reading experience, and find it online: maps, images, vocabulary, video, etc. You might even include brief articles to explain needed nonfiction content. Keep those pages open on a tab in your browser.
3. Next, using your preferred QR code generator, create a QR code for each of the resources you found.
4. Paste each newly generated QR code into your bookmark and add a title.
5. Print out the bookmarks for students and ensure they have a QR reader on their favorite device for easy access while reading.

It may seem daunting to create bookmarks like this for all the books in your library, but a little bit of teamwork goes a long way. Share your bookmarks with other teachers, and house them on a shared drive for easy access. Each time a colleague creates a bookmark, upload it to the shared drive for all to access. You might even gather a group of interested teachers together for an after-school bookmark-making session to fuel collaboration. And your students can join in, too! As they read, have them make lists of things in their books they wish they could see, hear, and view—and then use their lists as a starting point for creating additional bookmarks.

Outgrow Your Reading Life

I have learned many life lessons from the pages of a book, and one important lesson came from Dr. Seuss' *The Grinch Who Stole Christmas*. In this book, the curmudgeonly Grinch comes to realize the true meaning of Christmas (and, I would add, the true meaning of life) as his heart stretches larger and larger to accommodate the new emotions he is feeling. His previously two-sizes-too-small heart simply outgrows itself to fit his new way of living. I love the analogy of outgrowing ourselves: growing, changing, shifting, and challenging ourselves to be better versions of who we were yesterday. This same analogy works well for our reading hearts, and I'd argue that the best goal for our individual reading lives is to try and outgrow them: pushing our boundaries, challenging our thinking, and broadening our perspective of what is possible within the covers of a book—and the world.

Right now, think about the last five books you have read. Think about the characters, the setting, and the main events as you consider these questions:

- Are the characters similar? Are they the same gender, the same race, approximately the same age, and under similar circumstances?
- Are the settings similar? Do they share common locations (urban, suburban, or rural) and characteristics?
- How do the stories unfold? Are they typical fiction texts with a common theme? Do they follow the same kind of structure? Are they stories that end similarly?

If you answered "yes" to a majority of these questions, then you may have found yourself stuck in a reading rut, a clear sign that it is time to grow as a reader and diversify your text selections.

Imagine a Bigger Version of Your Reading Self

Chances are there's a predictability to the texts in your life: the many emails, your social media feed, your loved genres. But by surrounding yourself only with what feels comfortable, you are perpetuating a single story of your reading life that narrows your thinking, rather than expands it. Here are some ways to make changes:

- Choose an author you have not read before within your favorite genre. Ask colleagues for recommendations, browse Goodreads, or head to your local bookstore for suggestions.
- Choose a genre you wouldn't normally choose. Head online to search for recommended books and read other readers' reviews before making your selections.
- Choose a format you wouldn't normally choose. You might try reading a graphic novel or a collection of short stories, or you might listen to an audiobook.

- Choose a topic that will open your mind to new ideas. Read about geology, fashion design, the wonders of the world, or whatever speaks to you.

Small changes, such as those listed, can make a large difference in your reading life and in the lives of your students. Choose one, see how it makes you feel, and discover what you learn about yourself in the process.

Here's How to Bring It to the Classroom

Begin by having regular conversations about your reading lives with students and let them know that at one point or another, we might find ourselves in a reading rut: reading the same books in the same ways at the same times with little variation. Encourage your students to try new practices to stretch themselves as readers, and ensure that your classroom provides opportunities for this kind of experimentation.

Start with the Reading Without Walls Challenge created by Gene Luen Yang (2016), a former National Ambassador of Young People's Literature. The Reading Without Walls challenge has three components: read a book about a character who doesn't look like you or live where you live, read a book about a topic you don't know much about, and read a book written in a format you've never read before. This is a simple, yet effective, challenge that can begin any time of the year and continue as long as you like.

You might even keep the challenge going all year long and create a new challenge every month: read a new genre, read a new author, choose a new format, read a topic you know little about, read in a different location, read with someone you might not normally pair up with, etc. And while you could easily give students the same reading challenge, there is great power in creating personal challenges that have more meaning and potential impact. Students can choose personal goals and challenges that match their vision of their reading life and that will help them stretch their thinking. All you need is a willingness to try and a classroom that supports their risk-taking as readers.

Create a Reading Staircase

Our reading hearts have unlimited, boundless love. There is always room for one more character to meet, one more setting to experience, one more topic to learn. Each book we read has the opportunity to lead to the next one, if we just follow our hearts and kindle our interests, intentionally broadening our reading lives in the process. I like to think of this intentional kindling of our reading hearts through the analogy of a staircase, taking deliberate steps to stretch our hearts by linking our text selections together. Try this:

1. Turn to a fresh page in your reading notebook and draw an outline of a staircase.
2. Label the bottom step with the title of the most recent book you have finished reading.
3. Think about what interested you as you read: the characters? the format? the genre? the writing craft?
4. Next, find the title of a book that will help expand your reading life in that area. Write the title and the author's name on the next step and read the book.
5. Repeat. Each time you read a book, think about an aspect of the book that intrigued you and that you want to know more about. Use that understanding to find your next book and slowly stretch your reading heart over time.

While reading random books recommended online or by friends or family is certainly enjoyable, becoming intentional in our selections opens up deeper reflection around our reading lives. As you consciously kindle your reading interests, you'll likely become more and more comfortable opening your reading heart to something new. This experience will inevitably impact all aspects of living and learning in the world—because when we outgrow our reading lives, we outgrow ourselves. Our reading lives literally change the way we see the world. So while every reader deserves books that mirror their own life experiences, it is just as important, if not more, to read books that stretch our thinking, connect us to new ideas, disrupt our understandings, and provide new perspectives to consider.

Here's How to Bring It to the Classroom

Creating reading staircases in your classroom can have the same impact on your students. You might begin by creating a staircase for the read-alouds and class novels you bring into your classroom. This will help you become more intentional about your selections over time and ensure that you are providing connected reading experiences for your students.

Students could also create their own personal reading staircases on a page of their notebook to help them think intentionally about the books they choose for independent reading. Examples of reading staircases are shown in Figure 3.7.

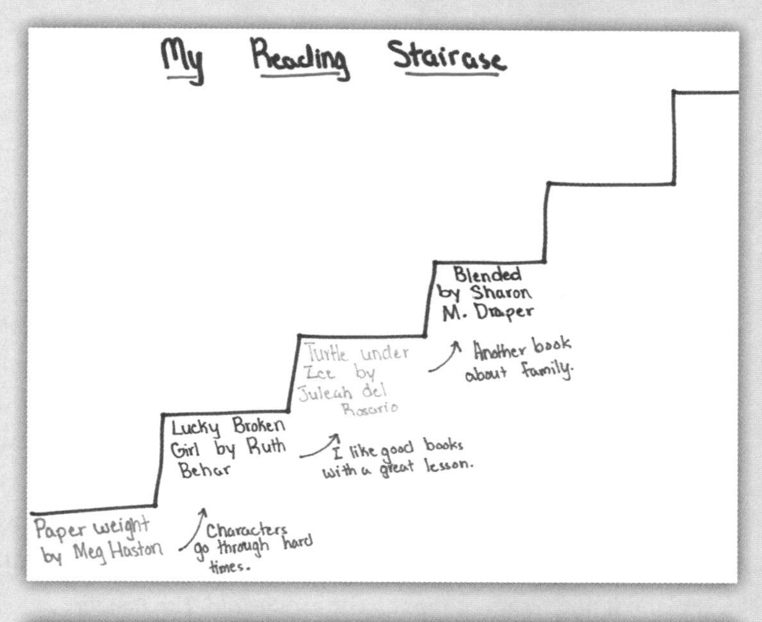

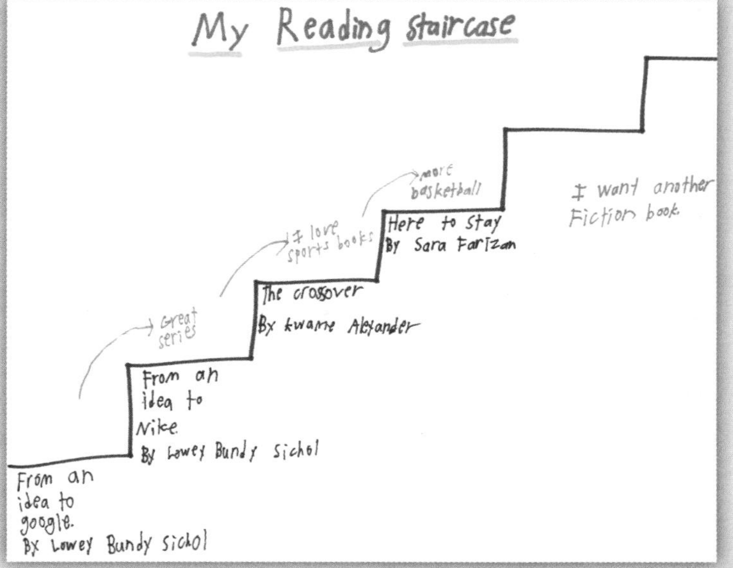

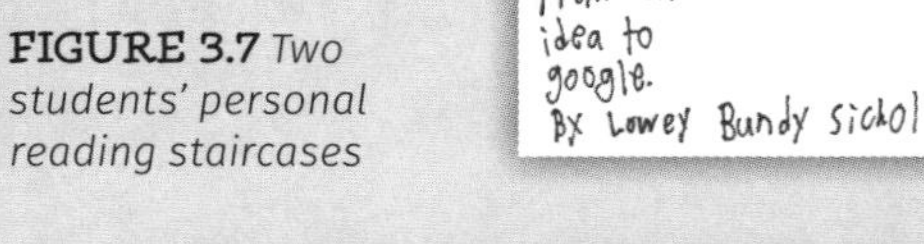

FIGURE 3.7 *Two students' personal reading staircases*

Crowdsource Your Collections

Crowdsourcing is a way to get information or advice from a large number of people, using the Internet. Wondering what to do in the city you're visiting? Ask Facebook. Looking for a new recipe to try? Head to Pinterest. In today's times, we can easily solicit the advice of others. So, why not use that to our advantage and crowdsource a collection of books that will move us out of our comfort zones? Here are a few ways to get started based on your favorite social media platform:

- Start with a personal post on your favorite social media platform asking for recommendations on your next book to read.
- Add in hashtags to get your post noticed, such as #TBRStack, #NeedABook, #WhattoReadNext.
- Tag in those that can help: your favorite publishers, authors you admire, fellow readers, and colleagues. My favorites? The International Literacy Association, The National Council of Teachers of English, the American Library Association, The ProjectLIT Community, and We Need Diverse Books, to name a few.

You might be surprised by how many recommendations you receive from your request—because readers help readers. Take note of the titles that are suggested and watch for those that are continually recommended. When I gave this a try, my fellow readers repeatedly suggested *The Benefits of Being an Octopus* by Ann Brayden. So, I read it and, honestly, have yet to read another book that has impacted me so profoundly on so many levels as an adult reader.

You might also take advantage of the crowdsourced collections that have already been curated for you. A variety of organizations provide booklists of current, diverse selections. These lists are organized by grade levels, topic, award winners, and more. Figure 3.8 offers a few of my favorite sites for keeping up-to-date.

Book List	Website Address
Where to Find Diverse Books	diversebooks.org/resources/where-to-find-diverse-books
Culturally Responsive Books	www2.ncte.org/blog/2016/04/culturally-responsive-books
Diversity in Graphic Novels	www2.ncte.org/blog/2018/08/diversity-graphic-novels
ILA Choices Reading Lists	www.literacyworldwide.org/get-resources/reading-lists
NCTE's Build Your Stack	www2.ncte.org/build-your-stack

FIGURE 3.8 *A few of my favorite sites for booklists*

☙ Here's How to Bring It to the Classroom ❧

When you crowdsource your next book to read, you're opening your reading life up to new possibilities only made possible by connecting with other readers. And you can provide the same for your students. Here are two of my favorite ways to replicate adult crowdsourcing with students:

- I Have—Who Has: This is a spin on the familiar game often played as a way to review skills and facts. In this version, students share the book they are reading and then ask for recommendations. A student might say, "I am reading *Front Desk* by Kelly Yang. Mia Tang's parents are immigrants who run a hotel and Mia helps her family in many ways. I really like how brave Mia is as she tries to help other immigrants and looks out for her family's future. Who has a book that has characters whose families are immigrants that I could read so I could learn more?" You could make this "game" part of your morning meeting or carve out time one day a week for students who are ready for a new book.
- Book Talks: Book talks elicit interest in new books by briefly showcasing the book's characters, setting, plot, lessons learned, and/or mood. Book talks can be simple conversations with other readers or more formal presentations that are recorded and compiled in a collection. You can start by simply connecting students with book talks that have already been created, such as Scholastic's collection of book talks. Once students are familiar with book talks, encourage them to create their own! They can share them with the class orally or even record them using Flipgrid. This way, students can access the book talks throughout the school year when they are ready for their next book.

Crowdsourcing recommendations for our next book to read not only provides us with books that are sure to not disappoint, they help us develop stronger connections with a larger community of readers, a community that can fuel our reading lives and sustain our reading spirits.

CHAPTER 4

Strengthen Our Reading Communities

When I was young, I participated in the summer reading challenge at my local library. In this challenge, readers set a goal to read a particular number of books throughout the summer and earned certificates and prizes along the way. I vividly remember the numerous trips my grandmother made back and forth to the library to keep up with my pace of reading. On one of those days, I walked up to the librarian to document my newly read titles, and instead of simply writing them down on my list of completed books, she asked me for a brief summary instead. I was stunned. No other librarian had asked me about the books I had read, so I was rather unprepared. Now, I had read the books and loved them all, but I was taken aback by her request. Why did I need to summarize the books? Didn't she believe that I read them? She must have seen the swirl of feelings on my face because she said, "Readers talk about books and I am curious about yours." Now, I imagine she really did want to know if I actually read *all* of those books each time I came in with my grandmother, but above that, she simply wanted to connect as a fellow reader. At that moment, my budding reading community was born. Sure, I talked to my friends and family about the books I was reading, but this was different. I was now talking to complete strangers about the books I was reading—and it mattered. Quite simply, I learned that readers seek out other readers to become part of a larger literate community. Readers

- make their reading lives visible in meaningful ways to share with others
- share their thinking to develop a collective understanding that surpasses our own
- recommend and review books so others might find their next book to read and so that they can do the same
- find ways to make reading a shared experience and develop relationships with other readers.

These outward readerly actions have sustained my reading identity over time, and over the years, I have come to learn a very important lesson: community promotes accountability. Sure, I have reading goals and standards for myself that I personally uphold, but when things get busy, it is my reading community that keeps me reading because I do not want to let them down. This kind of accountability is evident throughout all aspects of our life. Think about the times you want to hit snooze on your alarm rather than head to the gym, but knowing that your friends are there, waiting for you, pushes you to roll out of bed. As humans, we crave connection and meaning in our lives, and our reading lives are no different. Our reading communities provide a purpose and a meaningful audience for our reading lives, pushing us to become bigger versions of ourselves.

As I pause to reflect on my own reading communities and what they provide, I cannot help but realize that the connections and communities that fuel my work the most, the ones that truly ignite my energy and passion for reading, are comprised of readers whom I have never met. We don't talk about books over coffee or sip wine as we ponder our reactions to texts, and we don't gather for tasty snacks and snippets of literature (although I do love when that happens). No, instead, we update our Goodreads feeds in hopes of sharing them with each other. We tweet book recommendations and ask for books to add to our stacks through social media and clever hashtags. And while coffee, wine, and tasty snacks are completely enjoyable, they are not needed to sustain a nourishing reading community—only books and the occasionally funny gif are required.

Make Your Reading Life Visible

It is one thing to document our reading for ourselves, but it is quite another to share our reading lives with others. Think for a moment about how you make your reading life visible. Do you keep a personal list of titles? Do you showcase your books on a shelf? Do you share books read on social media? Do you use a digital book-sharing site to announce your status as a reader? Or, do you prefer to chat with a close friend or colleague? Regardless of how we do it, making our reading life visible matters. It matters greatly because we acknowledge our status as readers and invite connections with others based on our reading habits, interests, and inquiries.

Go Public with Your Stacks

Personal TBR stacks are often just that: personal. Books are stacked in our homes patiently waiting to be read to prompt a more consistent reading habit. But sharing those stacks with others fuels our sense of reading community.

I recommend that you start by sharing your stacks with your students. Choose a nook in your physical or online classroom and display the books you have finished reading. Each time you finish one, make a big deal of adding it to your stack and talk about other readers who might like to read it. You'll be surprised at just how quickly students ask to borrow them.

Looking for a way to attractively capture the titles you have read online instead? Create a digital bookshelf using tools like Padlet or Flipgrid. The tool you choose will depend on the purpose of your shelf. If you want a place to collect your completed books as images, then Padlet will work well for you. If you would like to go beyond the image and record a quick narration of your response and thinking around the book, then Flipgrid is a better choice.

On Padlet, you can create a digital shelf of the texts you have read and even create multiple bookshelves to house them by genre, reading rating, and more. Create a Padlet wall and choose the "shelf" option. Label your shelves to organize your texts: genre, date read, favorite authors, new books, etc. When you finish a book, add a new title to the appropriate shelf and label it with the title and author's name. Take a quick picture of the book cover and include yourself in the photo if you prefer shelfies (selfies with books) instead. Then, watch the wall fill with book covers over time as clear evidence of your reading life.

On Flipgrid, you might create book talks to document the books you are reading and the impact they are having on you. Book talks are brief descriptions of a text where the reader provides just enough information to draw in listeners and make them want to hear more. By recording book talks on Flipgrid, you can easily share your thinking with others. For inspiration, scan the QR code to find a Flipgrid where authors book-talk their own books.

https://bit.ly/2UlmyOh

Scan to visit the author connection Flipgrid page by Nicole Mancini

You'll find documenting your reading life digitally can provide you with the momentum you need to keep going. Plus, it will make sharing your titles with other readers a bit easier. And if you're up for another challenge, update your email signature with what you're reading, too!

Here's How to Bring It to the Classroom

Now that you've spent some time making your own reading life visible, think about how you can connect your efforts to the classroom. Do your students have opportunities to make their reading lives visible for others? Students could keep a list of their finished books in their reader's notebook, rate them with smiley faces or stars, and share them with their reading partners. Or, they could jot their titles on sticky notes and then post them on the classroom reading wall or on a bulletin board, with their names and/or pictures, or in some other special place. Figure 4.1 offers an example from Ms. Pipines' third-grade classroom.

FIGURE 4.1 *Ms. Pipines' classroom reading wall*

With the help of technology, you might create a digital reading wall on Padlet to showcase students' reading selections. Students can take a shelfie (a selfie with the book they've just completed reading) and list the title and author of the book to share with classmates. You'll find an example of a basic digital reading wall in Figure 4.2.

Stephanie Affinito • 2mo

Digital Reading Wall

You Go First by Erin Entrada Kelly ♡ 0 Add comment	**The Benefits of Being an Octopus** by Ann Braden ♡ 0 Add comment	**Clean Getaway** Nic Stone ♡ 0 Add comment	**Louisiana's Way Home** by Kate DiCamillo ♡ 0 Add comment	**Caterpillar Summer** by Gillian McDunn ♡ 0 Add comment
Prairie Lotus by Linda Sue Park ♡ 0 Add comment	**Some Places More Than Others** by Renee Watson ♡ 0 Add comment	**Extraordinary Birds** by Sandy Stark-McGinnis ♡ 0 Add comment	**Book Uncle and Me** by Uma Krishnaswami ♡ 0 Add comment	**Guts** by Raina Telgemeier ♡ 0 Add comment

FIGURE 4.2 *An example of a digital reading wall on Padlet*

Celebrating the books we have finished reading is wonderful, but our progress as readers matters just as much. So, why not make that progress visible too? Start by modeling it for students and then invite them into the process by having a different student create a display each week:

- Carve out a space in your classroom where you can easily display three books in a row. You might choose to prop books on the ledge of the whiteboard or display them on top of a filing cabinet with display easels.
- Assign a label to each book based on your reading progress: "Just Finished Reading," "Currently Reading," or "Reading Next." These phrases could be written above the books on the whiteboard or written on a card if displaying the books another way.
- Update your display often as you finish your books, and don't be afraid to have more than one book on display for what you are hoping to read next.
- Add a sticky note to the cover, making your thinking about the book visible. Write what you loved about the book you just finished, jot a note about what you are currently reading, and share why you are considering the book for your next read. Use this space to showcase not only titles, but also the ways readers think about their reading lives. Figure 4.3 offers an example from a sixth-grade class.

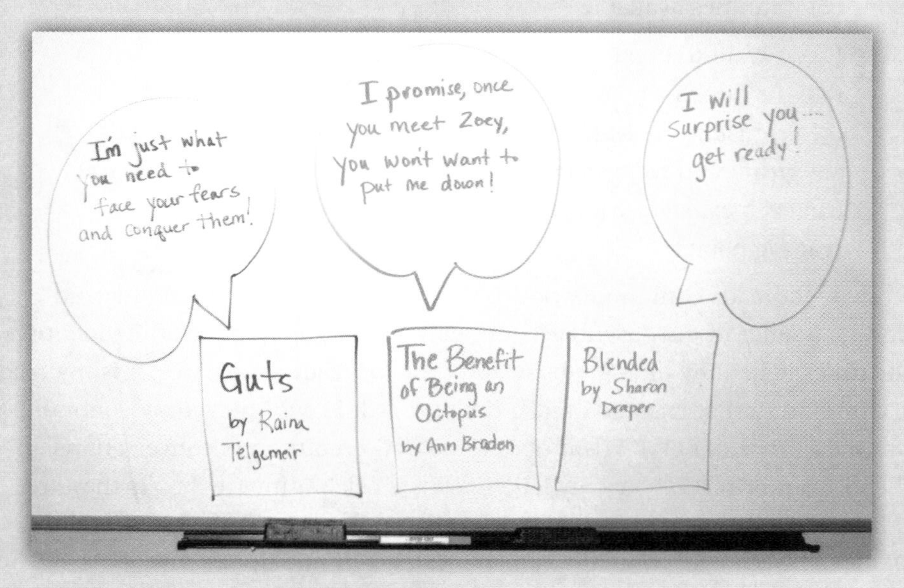

FIGURE 4.3 *A whiteboard book display*

Connect with Readers on Goodreads

Goodreads is a social platform that allows readers to connect with other readers. On Goodreads, readers share the books they are reading, find book recommendations, and discuss their reading with others. If you are not on Goodreads yet, here is your invitation to join. If you are, here are a few ways you might strengthen your participation in that community:

- First, if you have not yet done so, create an account and update your profile so other readers can learn more about you and your reading preferences.
- Update your shelves. Take some time to share your most recently completed texts and add a few titles to your "Want to Read" shelf. Update the book you are currently reading as well.
- Connect with fellow readers. Search for friends and family that might already have accounts. Then, connect with other readers who are reading the same books as you to broaden those with whom you book-talk.
- Join a reading group! There are many active book clubs on Goodreads for you to explore. Find a group reading the same book you are or search for your next read based on the communities available.
- If you want to open up another level of Goodreads, be sure to rate the books you are reading, mark your favorite genres, and create custom shelves. This information will unlock Goodreads' algorithm and recommend books based on your preferences. You can even evaluate your statistics as a reader and analyze your reading habits.

My Goodreads community nourishes and sustains my reading life and gives me a sense of purposeful accountability to maintain my reading identity. Sometimes, when my days are busy and time for reading is scarce, it is my reading community that ensures I make time to read. How? My reading community gives me a sense of FOMO (fear of missing out) on our book conversations. When I hear (or read about) my fellow readers celebrating the books they are reading, it sparks me to join the conversation right along with them. And this FOMO can work exceptionally well for students in our classrooms.

Here's How to Bring It to the Classroom

Students do not need their own Goodreads accounts to experience the benefits of a reading community. Carve out regular time during the day to update their status as readers. But if you'd like to give a digital platform a try, consider Biblionasium. Biblionasium is a social reading platform created specifically for students to share their reading lives with classmates, friends, and family. Students can make their reading life visible, exchange book recommendations with others, and interact with fellow readers online.

Analyze Your Reading Life

I am a self-proclaimed book nerd, and I know that many of you reading this are, too. If you are, then you might appreciate taking a hard look at your reading life in a very quantitative way. Analyze your reading life by geeking out on the mathematical statistics that not only make your reading life visible but also teach you a great deal about the messages it sends in the process.

I first learned about this technique from One Little Library (Curry 2019), and although I was a bit hesitant to invest the time and effort needed to truly analyze my reading life, I was certainly glad that I did so. I think you will be, too. Here's how to get started:

1. First, choose your spreadsheet platform. I prefer Google Sheets, but Microsoft Excel and Numbers can work just as well for this.
2. Next, decide what aspects of your reading life you want to analyze. Here are a few possibilities: genre, format, author's sex or gender identity, author's race, representation of characters, book setting, your rating, and abandoned books. Basically, you can decide to track any aspect you hope to get more insight into. Keep in mind that you can start small and add to your tracker over time.
3. Create your spreadsheet. Your first two columns should represent the book title and author, and I recommend freezing them there for easy comparison. Then, add columns based on the aspects of your reading life you hope to analyze. You'll also want to add

formulas to help you easily total the columns at the bottom. Think about the target number of books you hope to read in a single year, and then insert that many rows to remind you of your goal. Take a look at my simple sheet in Figure 4.4.

https://bit.ly/2UwPcMr

Scan to make a copy of my template

4. Lastly, feel free to personalize your spreadsheet! Color-code your columns to help you easily focus on what matters most to you, and choose fonts that represent your personality. If you would like to give this a try, but creating your own spreadsheet seems a bit daunting, then go ahead and make a copy of mine. Scan the QR code to make a copy to save to your Google Drive.
5. Next, enter your data. If you are as nerdy as I am, you'll want to reflect back on your reading life and enter data to analyze immediately. If not, vow to start documenting your reading life in this way from this point forward.
6. Then, let the reflecting begin! View the graphs automatically generated by the tool you chose to create your spreadsheet. How many books did you read in each genre? How many were written by new authors or authors who are BIPOC? How many books did you abandon? How many five-star ratings did you give? This is where the power of hard data comes to life: it allows you to see, and reflect on, the messages your reading life is sending. Is it telling a story you want it to tell?

If spreadsheets aren't your thing, try Google Forms instead. Create a Google Form with questions that match the aspects of your reading life that you hope to analyze. Each time you finish a book, complete your own survey and enter the needed information in your Google Form. This way, you can focus only on the book at hand and not have to see the volume of information that may be entered.

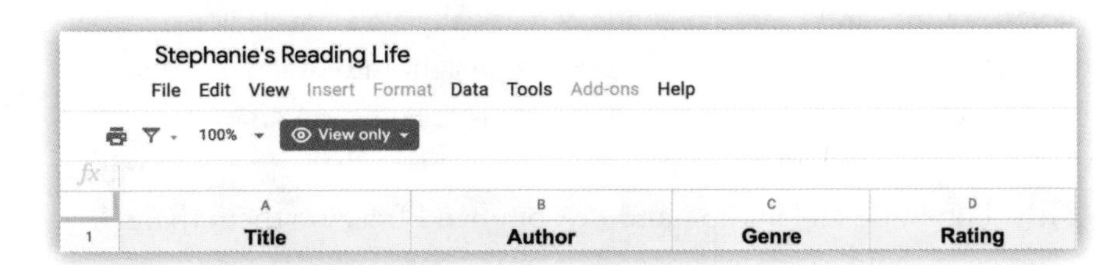

FIGURE 4.4 *A sample reading spreadsheet template*

Take a look at my own Google Form in Figure 4.5 and create your own to match your reading life and personality. You can still reflect on the data in the exact same way, but you might find this to be a more pleasant entry point.

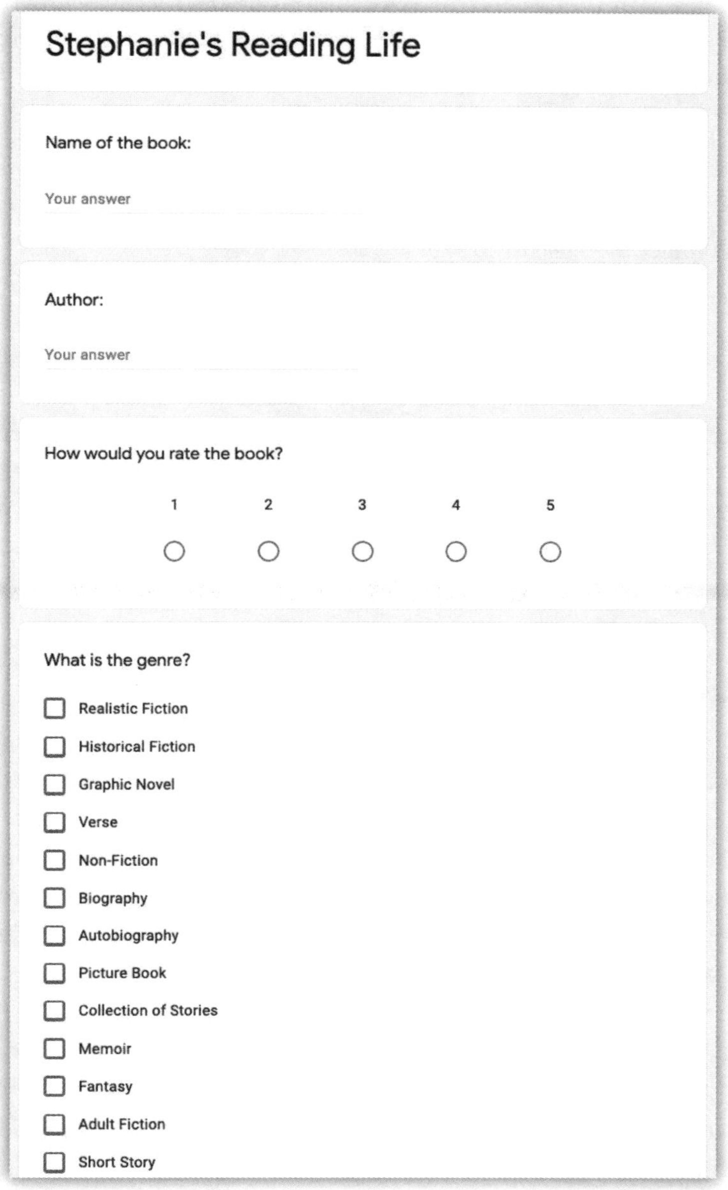

Stephanie's Reading Life

Name of the book:

Your answer

Author:

Your answer

How would you rate the book?

1 2 3 4 5

What is the genre?

- Realistic Fiction
- Historical Fiction
- Graphic Novel
- Verse
- Non-Fiction
- Biography
- Autobiography
- Picture Book
- Collection of Stories
- Memoir
- Fantasy
- Adult Fiction
- Short Story

FIGURE 4.5 *A screenshot of my Google Form to record the books I've read*

☙ Here's How to Bring It to the Classroom ❧

Students also benefit from analyzing and reflecting on their own reading lives over time, whether they keep a list of finished books, snap a shelfie on Padlet, record a video on Flipgrid, or showcase their titles on a Google Form. Regardless of the method they used, students can reflect on their reading lives, using the following questions:

- How many books did I read?
- What genres did I choose to read?
- What topics did I choose to read about?
- How did I feel about the books I read?
- Did I abandon any books? Why?
- Did I meet the reading goal I set for myself?

Reflecting on these questions offers students a starting point to look back on the titles they read, think carefully about their reading lives, and set new goals to continually develop their reading identities.

Broaden Your Reading Circles

Appreciation for circles has been traced back to forty thousand years ago, and circles remain a dominant shape in our world, from architecture to art. I find the circle to be a useful metaphor for thinking about reading communities. Merriam-Webster (2020a) defines *circle* as a "group of persons sharing a common interest or revolving about a common center." Reading communities literally enclose circles of readers together to focus on common interests of books, readers, and reading. I invite you to think about the reading communities you are part of by considering your reading circles.

Grab a piece of paper or your reader's notebook and draw a picture of yourself in the center of a new page (stick figures welcome). Next, draw a circle around yourself and label the circle with your closest reading connections. Who do you talk to about books most often? Colleagues? Friends? Then, draw another wider circle around the first and label it with the readers you connect with outside of your trusted inner circle of readers. Your local librarian? Your favorite bookseller? Readers from your book club? Finally, draw a third circle around your entire image and label it with the readers you connect with around the world. Colleagues you met through Twitter? Publishers you follow on social media? Fellow booklovers on your favorite reading platform?

Now, reflect on your reading circles. Here are three things to consider:

- Which circle of reading connections was the most robust?
- Which community circle might need a bit of a boost?
- What goals might you set for yourself to broaden your reading communities?

Ask: "What Are You Reading Lately?"

We all have our favorite sayings: *It is what it is. That's the way the cookie crumbles. You get what you get and you don't get upset.* We may be known for these sayings and unconsciously use them often. What's mine? You already know it: *So, what are you reading lately?* This question inevitably sneaks into my conversations with unsuspecting partners (I'll never forget the priceless look on the face of a fifth grader on summer vacation when I casually asked this question over dessert). It is a simple, yet highly effective technique for getting reading ideas that I encourage you to try tomorrow. Better yet, try it today. Here are a few possibilities:

- Ask the first person you see after reading this.
- Call up a family member to ask this important question.
- Text a friend to learn more about their current title.
- Ask a colleague during your lunch break or while waiting for a faculty meeting to begin.

These are all easy, but impactful, ways to connect with fellow readers and learn about the books they are reading. But if we stay within our current reading circles, then we will have little opportunity to broaden them. So, try asking that same question to someone outside of those circles:

- Email a friend or colleague you haven't seen in a while and ask for a recommendation.

- Ask the cashier at the next drive-through window you pass through.
- Turn to a fellow coffee drinker while waiting in line and learn about the book they're currently reading.
- Feeling feisty? Ask the next telemarketer who calls your home to share a title before you listen to their request.

You might initially feel a bit odd posing this question to others, but you might also be surprised at what you learn about the fellow readers around you, especially your students.

Here's How to Bring It to the Classroom

Make *So, what are you reading lately?* your mantra with students—that way, they will expect it and continuously think about their reading life so they can share it with you. I'll never forget the time my son and I were walking through a store and spotted his fourth-grade teacher. He hid behind me for a moment and said, "Wait! I've got to remember the title of the book I am reading before I see Mrs. Wiekierak!" Years had passed since the fourth grade, but she had made a big impression on his identity as a reader. Challenge your students to adopt this phrase as well, asking their friends and family members what they are reading, too!

Connect with Reading Partners

Partnerships fuel all aspects of our lives. Want to lose weight? Get a workout buddy. Want to learn to paint? Grab your bestie and head to a painting party. While we can make strides in our lives on our own, having someone by our side to inspire and support our actions can make a world of difference. Our reading lives are no different.

One of the best pieces of advice I can give to strengthen your reading community is to find a reading partner: a fellow reader who is ready and willing to talk books, swap titles, and kibbitz about the contents. I'm not alone in this advice. Anne Bogel (2018), author of *I'd Rather Be Reading: The Delights and Dilemmas of the Reading Life,* urges readers to find their reading twin, someone whose own reading life resembles their own to share titles, offer new reading experiences, and even steer them away from books they might have ultimately abandoned.

Finding a reading partner can be as simple as turning to a good friend or close family member. Chances are that if they are present in your life, they also feel the same about books and reading as you do. And if not, connecting together around books can help broaden both of your lives by sharing favorite selections. But reading partnerships need cultivating. Make a regular habit of reaching out to your reading partner to

- share the titles you are reading and want to read next
- talk about your individual titles and how they are shaping your thinking
- lift compelling lines from the text to share with each other
- share personal reading goals and help hold each other accountable for reaching them
- plan to read the same text together and discuss.

You can broaden your reading partnerships to book clubs as well. Chances are you have participated in a book study around a professional text with colleagues. But, when was the last time you participated in a book club around a text you have chosen to read purely for pleasure? Growing up, I thought book clubs were reserved for English class where I was forced to meet with a group of students to talk about novels assigned to the class. It wasn't until I was introduced to Oprah's book clubs that I realized this was something that readers actually did on purpose and with gusto. Here are three ways to get started:

- Join a local book club that meets regularly. Start by asking at your local library or bookstore to learn about active groups.
- Form your own! Gather together interested readers and choose a common text to read. Set a schedule, arrange a location, and meet regularly.

- Participate in an online book club. Join in on Oprah's book club, find one that fits your interests on Goodreads, or find one on social media. My favorite sites are Booksparks (http://linktr.ee/booksparks) and Barnes and Noble Book Club (www.barnesandnoble.com/h/book-club).

https://bit.ly/3ks6dlE

Scan to learn more about silent book clubs

You might find it hard to add yet another activity to your busy days and weeks, so a silent book club might work better for you. What's a silent book club, you ask? Silent book clubs (silentbook.club), founded by Guinevere de la Mare and Laura Gluhanich, invite readers to read in companionable silence while indulging in a beverage or chosen snack. While there's lively discussion initially, the bulk of the time is spent reading, giving yourself the time and community to simply read together. Learn more by scanning the QR code.

Here's How to Bring It to the Classroom

We often create reading partnerships for our students because we see the benefits first-hand. Partnerships boost reading identity, support fluency and comprehension, strengthen community, foster a collective understanding of a book, open our minds to new perspectives and ways of thinking, and renew our sense of shared wonder around text. Try one of the following and see how it boosts the community of readers in your classroom:

- Develop reading partnerships. Pair students together to talk about their reading lives. They can share titles, hold each other accountable for their goals, and discuss their growing understandings. Scholastic (2019) has a great collection of resources to help you get started. Scan the QR code for additional information.

https://bit.ly/2UmR8qS

Scan to explore Scholastic's resources on reading partnerships

- Connect reading buddies. Connect readers together across classrooms to build more-diverse connections. You can partner with a fellow grade-level colleague or reach out to other grade levels for cross-grade conversations.
- Form book clubs around common texts. Showcase the available titles and encourage interested students to join in.

- Offer book clubs around independent-reading selections. Book clubs do not have to be defined by a common text. Connect students together around their independent-reading selections to learn from each other and add titles to their to-be-read stacks.

Any attempt to connect readers together, no matter how small, has the potential to boost students' reading identities and spark authentic motivation for reading.

Start a Book Relay

I first learned about book relays from Jill Davidson, a literacy coordinator in Canada and cocreator of #shelfietalk with Kim Stewart. She created a book relay in her district to increase access to new and diverse texts and to strengthen teachers' reading communities over her districts' geographical boundaries. And now, you can, too! Here's how it works:

1. Teachers are grouped into teams of five or six, and the relay works very much like a chain letter.
2. Each member of the team receives a different book and has four to six weeks to read it.
3. As teachers read, they are encouraged to share their thinking with the next reader of the book on a sticky note.
4. When finished, teachers send the book and the sticky note to the next person on the list.
5. Teachers receive a new book from a fellow colleague, and the cycle continues until everyone in the group has read all the books (five or six books, depending on the number of participants).
6. At the end, teachers receive the book they started with, along with the sticky notes from the other readers in the group. Teachers celebrate the completion of the relay with a group session to discuss the books together.

Sounds fun, right? So, why not create a book relay of your own? Start small and gather a colleague or two together and create a relay team. Or, send out an email to your colleagues and see who is up for trying something new! Scan the QR code for a basic email template to personalize.

https://bit.ly/3lDKbNW

Scan for a book-relay email template

The book relay is an innovative way to bring teachers together around books, ones they can share with their students. Not only can teachers connect with new readers across the district, they can learn from each other's thinking, too.

Here's How to Bring It to the Classroom

While this book relay began within a single district of teachers, there are tremendous possibilities for creating book relays with your students. Here are a few to consider:

- Read-Aloud Relay: Introduce your students to the idea of a book relay by relaying read-aloud titles with other classrooms in the school. Elicit your librarian's help to gather together memorable titles to read, discuss, and pass onto the next classroom.
- New-Books Relay: Once students understand how a book relay works, offer interested students a chance to participate in one. This works especially well when introducing a set of new books to the class that multiple students want to get their eyes on. Share your new titles with students and give a short book talk to generate interest. Create a relay group with the same number of students as books, and decide how long each student will have to read their book and who they will pass it to. This is a great way to watch new books ripple through the class!
- Thematic Relay: Thematic relays offer students the chance to explore texts connected around a common theme. Gather together a few titles of different genres, but the same general topic. Create a relay group of students interested in exploring the topic more deeply, and find the time for them to meet periodically to talk about their developing understandings.
- Genre Relay: Genre relays invite students to explore a genre in greater depth. Begin with a minilesson or two on the characteristics of a particular genre, and gather a few texts together. Create a relay group of students excited to explore the genre and share their learning with others.

Book relays offer students an innovative way to connect together as a community of readers and do not have to stay within your classroom walls. Reach out to other classrooms interested in relaying together within your school or district, and consider joining with classrooms across your state and even the country through social media.

Connect with Authors and Illustrators

When I was a young reader, I wrote letter after letter to my favorite authors, hoping to earn a response. After months of checking my mailbox every day, I might only receive a standard postcard, but it sent my enthusiasm for reading through the roof. And, honestly, not much has changed since then. I get the same kind of electric charge each time I connect with a beloved author as an adult. Readers become so entangled in the pages of their books that we feel a kinship with the characters and a true connection with the authors and illustrators. Strengthening those connections, either in person or virtually, can skyrocket our enthusiasm for reading.

Be Inspired by Author Backstories

You've learned in the opening pages of this book how important stories are in my life: reading them, writing them, living them. I use them to make sense of the world, to make sense of my own life, and to become inspired to write my own. And I use the backstories of authors, the ones that describe how they became the authors they are today, to spark a more inspired reading (and writing!) life.

I invite you to choose an author you love, investigate their backstory, and let it spark your own reading life. Here are a few ways to do just that:

- Read the book jacket. Many readers turn to the book jacket for a sneak peek into the contents of the book, but I love reading the author biography even more. Getting a glimpse into the author's life gives me even more appreciation for their efforts in writing the book so that it can change the way I think and feel about the world.
- Browse their website. Most authors have a personal website to share their stories, extend invitations to connect, and offer readers additional ways to engage with the text.
- Seek interviews and/or podcasts. Start by listening to *The Children's Book Podcast* (https://lgbpodcast.libsyn.com) or *The Yarn* (https://podcasts.apple.com/us/podcast/the-yarn/id1028877816) to learn more about your favorite authors and to become inspired by the stories of authors you have yet to read.
- Google it. Yes, google it. Simply type in the words *how did [x] become an author.* This is how I learned that Kate DiCamillo worked many odd jobs before finally committing to her writing

> and that she faced over four hundred rejection letters before publishing her first book. It's also how I learned that Aisha Saeed loves Redwood trees because of the sense of joy and wonder they bring, which prompted me to try reading outside more often. So, go ahead and google your favorite author and see what might inspire your reading life, too!

It might seem odd that learning the backstories of the authors you are reading could boost your sense of reading community, but connecting with authors around their stories has tremendous power to link us together in a larger community of readers. And that kind of connection can catapult a young reader into a robust reading life, too.

Here's How to Bring It to the Classroom

Encourage your students to learn about the backstories of their favorite authors. They can use the same strategies you used to discover the stories of your favorite authors, but I highly recommend that you read and share with them *Our Story Begins: Your Favorite Authors and Illustrators Share Fun, Inspiring, and Occasionally Ridiculous Things They Wrote and Drew as Kids* (Weissman 2018). This book is a compilation of short essays written by beloved children's authors about their childhood and their journeys to become authors. You and your students will love the candid, inspiring stories within the pages. Encourage students to write their own backstories as a way to build their own sense of reading and writing identity. They might include how, when, and why they became a reader, their favorite books and genres, and memorable books throughout their reading lives.

Seek Out Author Events

I love meeting my favorite authors and, better yet, meeting new authors whose books I have yet to read, fueling my reading enthusiasm forward. Connect with authors in any way you can: in person, virtually, or through social media. Here are four options to jump-start your calendar of author events:

- Ask your local librarian. Many libraries host author events for members to enjoy, often free!
- Connect with local bookstores. They are sure to have multiple events showcasing the work of authors. Look for your favorites, but be open to meeting new authors to explore as well.
- Find virtual opportunities. Many publishing companies offer virtual visits and webinars with their authors. Sign up for their newsletters and be on the lookout for those events.
- Watch the replay. I love KidLit TV, the place to discover great children's books and connect with the people who create them. Head to their website, find treasured authors, and learn more about them directly from the authors themselves!

Here's How to Bring It to the Classroom

There are many ways to invite authors into your school to inspire your reading community. The Society of Children's Book Writers and Illustrators Speaker's Bureau (www.scbwi.org/speakers-bureau) has a comprehensive list of authors who offer school visits. It even allows you to search by state and by the recommended age range for their books. Publishers typically list their authors who are available for school and Skype visits on their websites, so start with your favorite publisher and see what you can find. And you can always google authors and find additional information on their websites.

If you'd like something more in-depth and sustained, then explore an inspiring Twitter feed celebrating authors connecting with classrooms: #KidsNeedMentors. In this initiative, authors are paired with classrooms for an entire school year to connect, collaborate, and learn together through virtual meetings and social media. Authors share books and inspiration, and fuel students' reading hearts—and students do the same. Are you interested in the program? Head online to #KidsNeedMentors and start scrolling. You won't be sorry you took a look!

Connect on Social Media

While nothing can replace the thrill of meeting admired authors in person, receiving a reply from them on Twitter, or even just a like for one of my tweets, sends me into fits of happiness. I urge you to use social media to create live connections with your treasured authors, particularly on Twitter and Instagram.

https://bit.ly/3lsbXx3

Scan to view Heinemann's Twitter for Educators *webinar*

Let's start with Twitter. If you don't have a Twitter account, you'll need to create one. Heinemann has a wonderful (and free) webinar on Twitter for educators that you can check out by scanning the QR code.

Start with the most recent book you have read and search for the author on Twitter. Snap a picture of the book and add a message to your tweet. You might simply state that you are currently reading the book and enjoying it, or you can share how it is impacting you as a reader. Tag the author in the tweet and send it off.

I use Instagram to connect with authors, snap and share pictures of the books I am reading, update the locations I am reading them, and even offer pages that are personally meaningful to me. Here's a step-by-step breakdown so you can do the same:

1. If you do not yet have an account on Instagram, visit their website to create one with little hassle.
2. Using your mobile device, snap a picture of the book you are reading or take a picture of the page that lit your reading heart on fire.
3. Upload the photograph and add a personal message: you might tell where and when you are reading and what you're thinking about or pose a question about the text.
4. Add a hashtag. Social media, in general, seems to love hashtags, but I have found that Instagrammers especially love the hashtag. So, add one (or three!) to your post, for example: #ReadingintheCar, #JustOneMorePage, #BookNerd, #CannotPutItDown, #YouHaveToReadThis.

Many authors respond pretty quickly on both platforms, so get ready to experience the thrill of the connection. Then, repeat!

Here's How to Bring It to the Classroom

Once you have experienced this kind of reading exhilaration using social media for yourself, you'll want to bring it to your classroom. I promise. Head to your classroom Twitter or Instagram account and create a post sharing the book you are currently reading to or with your students. Tag the author and illustrator and even add the publisher, if you'd like. You might include a favorite line, note the students' reactions, or pose a question.

Regularly share your classroom feed with students and celebrate likes and responses. Create simple Twitter or Instagram templates, and invite students to draft your next post so they can share their reading with the broader social media community as well. If you're hesitant to create a social media profile for the class, display students' printed posts on a bulletin board in the classroom instead, replicating the feel of a social media feed. See Figure 4.6 for an example using Instagram.

FIGURE 4.6 *Instagram wall in Kristen Dembroski's classroom*

Section 2
Writing

Preface to Section 2

I am a writer. While this four-word sentence is a seemingly straightforward statement of my identity, it is hard won. You see, while I wholeheartedly believed in my abilities and identity as a reader right from the start, my identity as a writer has waxed and waned over the years. As a child, my first writing experience was a memorable one. I learned that if you moved colorful crayons over the surface of a large blank canvas, my cousin's bedroom wall, then the images and words in my head would spill beautifully out into the world, just as they had for Harold and his purple crayon. I remember being mesmerized by the images covering the wall and, in that moment, knew I had many stories to tell. Thankfully, I also had family members who weren't too upset at my masterpiece and showed me how to scrub the walls clean and use gleaming white paper instead.

Throughout my childhood, I learned that writing had power. I could make others happy by sharing my printed words. I spent hours at my grandparents' house creating a weekly newspaper with my best friend as we wrote feature articles and housekeeping columns, and even tried our hand at basic comics. That experience gave me the confidence I needed to write a letter to my local editor in response to a piece in our weekly newspaper on discrimination of disabled people. Seeing my words in print, in a real newspaper, brought me great satisfaction and joy. My voice was heard.

As I grew older, I turned to writing to help me conquer an illness that left me out of school for years with little energy to do anything except think and write. The poems I created to work through my frustration, fear, and depression kept me going in those lonely times, and I learned that writing had another power: to heal.

But as I returned to school and, eventually, college, I lost touch with the power that writing once had for me. I filled my time writing reading responses and educational essays that interested me but did not set my writing on fire. I learned new genres of writing, too, such as case reports and research critiques. It was hard work and pushed me out of my comfort zone, but it felt good to remember the satisfaction of giving everything I had to the writing process. So, you can imagine my reaction when those papers were consistently returned with red comments filling the pages, clearly belittling the effort I had put into them. I'd like to tell you that this experience fired me up, challenged me to rise to the occasion, and spurred me to the next phase in my writing career. But, it didn't. Instead, it made me doubt my writing abilities and question all the power I had felt growing up as a writer. Sure, I continued in my studies and, eventually, my papers were returned with less and less red scratched across the page, but the experience haunted me. It would be years before I picked up a pen and put it to paper simply because I wanted to. I lost touch with who I was as a writer, and this impacted how I approached writing in my classroom.

It wasn't until I started my master's degree that I let myself revisit my old identity as a writer. I had the honor of listening to Lucy Calkins speak at a local workshop and spent the day soaking in her words and inspiration. I left that day determined to bring that same fire for writing back to my fourth-grade classroom but knew I would first need to bring that fire back to myself. I dug through my old journals and pieces of writing and reminisced, reminding myself I really was a writer. And I started writing again—small entries in my notebook, newsletters for my students, and shared stories in our classroom writing workshop. I knew firsthand the power a teacher's words could have on students' identities and worked to cultivate, not condemn, my students' writing lives. While I had much to learn, my re-emerging identity as a writer fueled my own writing and writing instruction.

As I continued in my career, I realized that many of my colleagues shared the same hesitation about their writing identities and their ability to teach writing well. In our classrooms, we were focusing on formats and formulas to help our students succeed on school tasks rather than on voice and choice to empower them as writers. It took me a great deal of time, writing, and learning to realize that we could, in fact, accomplish both. And now, in my current position as a literacy teacher–educator and literacy coach, I work to help teachers reclaim their own writing lives to better support the teaching of writing in their classrooms.

When we allow ourselves to experience the expansive and transformative power that writing can have in our lives, or resurrect it from our early childhood experiences, we can't help but look at writing instruction with that same expansive and transformative lens. And when we do, we may realize that our lack of writing identity impacts the students in our classrooms. We may rely on formulas and formats to teach writing instead of sharing our work as writers with students. We may privilege checklists and rubrics on the products of writing—instead of on the process—to make sure students are well prepared. We may limit writing topics and formats out of a need to cover standards rather than to help students explore their lives And I get it. I did all of that and more. But once Lucy reminded me how important my own identity as a writer was to my students' success, I have been a work in progress ever since.

Now, picking up a pen or stroking the keys of a keyboard will not instantly change the way you feel about writing or how writing works in your classroom. But, giving yourself the time and space to reconnect with your writing life will prompt you to think differently about writing instruction in your classroom. You'll remember the joy that writing may have once held in your writing life. You'll experience the confidence that consistent writing can bring to all aspects of your life. You'll find connections between your reading life and writing life that make each stronger. And of course, along the way, you'll find connections to your classroom: aha moments in which you realize that small changes to your daily classroom routines can make a large difference, slower realizations that larger shifts could be made in the way you teach writing, opportunities to connect with your students as fellow writers, and experiences that can be life changing for students.

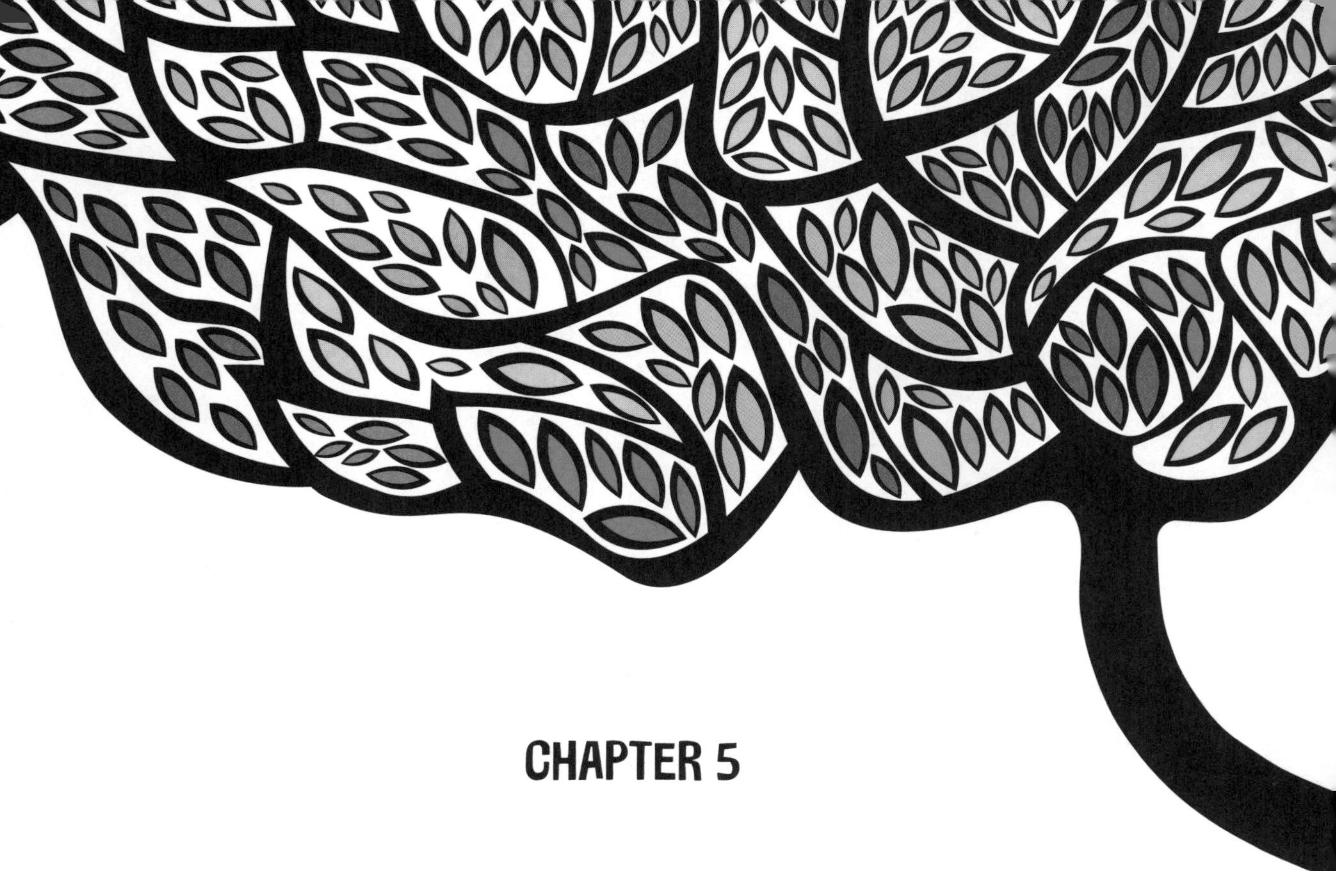

CHAPTER 5

Cultivate Our Writing Habits

In my experience, many educators find it easier to bring reading habits into their daily lives than they do writing habits. Sure, we write every day as adults, but the act of writing for no functional reason at all can be a harder habit to adopt. But once you have a better understanding of *why* a particular activity is good for you and your well-being, it is easier to make that activity a habit. And once you create a habit, you begin experiencing the benefits, making it easier to stay on track. This is called a keystone habit. First coined by Charles Duhigg (2012), *keystone habits* are small habits that we bring into our lives that often have a larger impact on our well-being. Take healthy eating, for example. If you consciously develop more healthful eating patterns, all aspects of your life are impacted: you feel better, sleep better, have a stronger immune system, and boost your overall well-being. Daily writing has the same domino effect on our daily lives. Writing can

- keep memory sharp
- boost overall mood and confidence
- evoke mindfulness and clarity
- help us reflect on events and experiences
- clear minds of feelings of anxiety or stress
- spark creativity
- promote gratitude.

If you are reading this book in order, you have already explored ways to make daily reading a priority in your life. Those same ideas will support your writing life as well. You might pair an old habit with a new habit and pick up your notebook as you sip your morning coffee or tuck yourself into bed at night. You might create a trip wire for yourself, a tangible reminder to write just a little bit each and every day. This might be a reminder on your phone, a sticky note on your laptop, or placing your notebook front and center where you will see it each day. You might even use a habit tracker to celebrate each day of writing. What better way to end the day than noting your writing accomplishments or making plans to write the next day?

But many teachers find it more intimidating to find the time to write than they do to read. With reading, we simply need to find a good book, a comfortable place to read, and ten minutes to get started. Easy. But writing can feel different. What do I write about? What if it isn't good enough? What if someone sees it? These questions haunt our writing lives—and not our reading lives.

Start a Writer's Notebook

I've had a special love of notebooks ever since I was a little girl. I carried them around with me, stuffed them into my backpacks and bags, and piled them throughout the house. I loved them in all shapes and sizes: large notebooks with lines for writing stories, smaller notebooks with blank pages for sketching and drawing, and miniature notebooks that I carried with me wherever I went to collect ideas and pass the time. Fast-forward thirty or so years later and not much has changed. I adore my notebooks and have several that I write in across a single day.

If I could share only one piece of advice to grow your writing life and develop a writing habit, it would be this: start a writer's notebook today. A writer's notebook is an indispensable tool for living a writerly life. It is a space to capture your thinking, collect observations and ideas, and plant seeds for future writing pieces. It can come in many formats, shapes, sizes, and colors, but the purpose is the same: to provide a powerful tool for writing and living (Fletcher 1996). My writer's notebook has been the single most important factor in developing my identity as a writer. Why? Because it prompts me to write every single day. Because it invites me to fill blank pages of paper with notes, ideas, sketches, and bursts of text. Because it helps me become a better observer of the world and of myself. Because it reminds me of the stories that are inside me just waiting to spill onto the pages even if they will never be seen by others. In short, my writer's notebook reminds me to be a writer, to write my life on the page. And now, I'm inviting you to do the same.

Choose Your Notebook

The first step is to choose your notebook. While a plain spiral notebook will do, your writer's notebook should be a prized possession, one that invites you to keep it close and draw, sketch, and write across the pages as if they were created just for you.

Take a few minutes to think about the kind of notebook that might fit your lifestyle, meet your individual needs, and set your writing heart on fire. Consider these questions:

- How large do you want your pages to be? Since you'll want to keep your writer's notebook close by, be sure to choose a size that will travel easily with you. My first rule is that my notebook *must* fit in my purse.
- Do you prefer blank paper, dotted paper, or lined pages? Honor your own needs and choose the kind of page that works for you.
- Where does the spiral edge suit you? At the top or on the side? Or, instead of a spiral, would you prefer a book spine or even a small binder filled with paper?
- Do you need the pages to be removable? While some writers are content to section off their notebook with sticky notes or

dog-eared pages, others prefer removable pages to organize and reorganize as the notebook evolves.

- How durable does your collection need to be? Busy teachers on the go often load materials and supplies in and out of bags and totes. If this is you, you might choose a notebook with a hard cover to keep up with your active lifestyle.
- Do you prefer digital paper and a stylus over the feel of a pen gliding across the page? If so, you might look into apps that allow you to create a digital writer's notebook instead.

Now, you might be thinking that I am going a bit over the top. How could this much thinking possibly go into choosing a notebook? While I do not want you to overthink it, I do want your notebook to be something that is highly personal to you, something that brings a smile to your face when you see it and begs you to fill the pages with your words and images.

- My own personal notebook is 5 by 8.25 inches, the perfect size to keep in my purse or school bag.
- It is not too thick. I love the feeling I get when I fill the last page of my notebook, a signal that I have indeed built my writerly life and it's time for yet another.
- It has a durable cover to withstand my busy lifestyle as well as a band to secure the pages together and keep them safe in my purse.
- It has blank pages. I absolutely, positively, must have blank pages in my notebook. I need the freedom to write and sketch in any direction that suits my mood and purpose for writing.

Many teachers choose to personalize their notebooks as well. Once you find the notebook that is just right for you, feel free to personalize the cover with photographs, quotes, clip art, and images that represent who you are. By doing so, you become truly invested in the notebook and gift yourself with something perfectly suited to you. If you own and honor your notebook, you can own and honor your writing.

☙ Here's How to Bring It to the Classroom ❧

Introducing a writer's notebook to students (Fletcher 1996; Ball 2018) gives them a space to explore writing, personal reactions, and reflections; a chance to practice writing strategies with little risk; and opportunities to set goals and work toward them. Linda Rief (2014) widens our vision of the notebook beyond a space to practice craft and to a space where students might also

- record, respond, and react to nightly reading by writing or drawing
- hold on to memories (whether they feel significant or relevant, insignificant or irrelevant)
- record thoughts, observations, and questions about their immediate world or the world at large
- question reading, writing, learning
- take out frustration, fear, anger, or sadness
- remember everything that makes them happy, makes them smile
- work out who they are by thinking about all that matters or doesn't matter to them
- keep ideas in one place so they don't lose their thinking
- establish the habits of collecting, noticing, listening, and writing.

What opportunities like those mentioned above do your students currently have to write freely and explore their sense of self and their place in the world? If you're wondering where to start, I urge you to get your hands on a copy of Ralph Fletcher's (1996) *A Writer's Notebook*. This book may be small, but it's packed full of ideas to help you show up to your writer's notebook. Fletcher (1996) offers a wide range of writing opportunities to get your pencil moving: small moments, seed ideas, mind pictures, snatches of talk, lists, memories, and more.

Invite students to choose a writer's notebook that suits their preferences, writing needs, and personalities. Use your own writing notebook as a model and share your rationale for choosing it, helping your students articulate their preferences as writers. Then, decide how to bring personalized notebooks directly to your students. We can do this in a few ways:

- Add writing notebooks to the students' supply list. If this list is sent out before the school year begins, provide students with guidance for how they might choose their notebooks. Or, wait until the school year begins to request the notebooks so that you can guide students to make decisions about which notebook would be best for each of them.
- Gather notebooks over time and present them to students. I love collecting notebooks. I scour the clearance aisles of my local office- and craft-supply stores to find notebooks of all shapes and sizes to use with teachers and students.
- Make one! If purchasing notebooks is not an option, then make them instead. Copy papers with various configurations of lines and spaces for drawing, and stack them on a table. Allow students to choose their favorite color of construction paper, the kind of paper they most want to write on, and an end page. The pages can be laminated for extra durability and then bound together for a handmade notebook.
- Get creative. You might ask your administrator if there is textbook money to purchase notebooks for your class or involve the parent–teacher association at your school. Many teachers have used Donors Choose as a way to obtain supplies for their classrooms; it can be a good way to get personalized journals into the hands of students.

These small acts of ownership have big implications for writers. Our writer's notebook is a portable writing space that can travel with us wherever we go and whenever inspiration strikes. Putting students in control of their own notebooks can be the first step to invite them to show up to the page.

Show Up to the Page

Many writers set a daily quota or word count to build a writing habit and consistently put pen to paper, even when the going gets tough. Kate DiCamillo vows to write two pages per day (about six to nine hundred words), while Stephen King and Nicholas Sparks reach for two thousand. And if you can believe it, Pintip Dunn strives to write five to ten thousand words daily! While I cannot imagine writing ten thousand words per day, I *can* imagine writing two or three hundred words daily. I might write in my notebook, draft a blog post, create teaching materials, and even rack up the words by writing in my gratitude journal. You see, the point of this writerly habit isn't the number of words set for a daily quota, it is the act of showing up to the page (or screen) each and every day.

Think for a minute about what being a writer means to you and how your notebook can help you get there. Does it mean writing daily in your notebook and feeling creative? Does it mean feeling calm as a result of journaling your thoughts and ideas? Do you want to share an aspect of your life by writing blog posts? Do you want to feel like you took a step toward your dream of writing a book? Or, do you want to connect with others through cleverly crafted social media posts instead? Then, decide how to show up to the page each day. Here are a few suggestions:

- Create a daily ritual signaling your brain that it is time to write. Brew a pot of coffee, gather your favorite notebook, or put on your fuzzy socks and head to your desk. Choose whatever works for you.
- Create a daily time to write and schedule an event on your calendar. Set a reminder so you won't break your writing date with yourself.
- Steal five minutes. Marcia Golub, author of *I'd Rather Be Writing* (1999), reminds us that the amount of time you write each day does not matter; the fact that you actually write something does. All that takes is five minutes of writing stolen throughout your day.
- Go rogue. Close your computer, turn your phone on airplane mode, and minimize other distractions, if you can. Set a timer and write for that entire time without interruption. Dedicate your whole self to the page and see what happens.
- Take your notebook with you. Don't create a safe space for your notebook at home. It should travel with you for whenever the mood or writing inspiration strikes.

- Celebrate your efforts. You can use a habit tracker (see more about this on page 29) or note your progress on a simple calendar. Each day, browse through your growing pages and soak the writing in.

Deciding how you will show up to the pages of your notebook is a highly personal decision, but a little planning and preparation can go a long way toward building daily writing habits. Choose one of the suggestions from the previous list and as Marcia Golub (1999) reminds us, "If you'd rather be writing, you can. It's as simple as that" (229).

Here's How to Bring It to the Classroom

Many classrooms set a minimum expectation for writing and track the amount of time students independently engage in writing each day, charting the minutes in celebratory fashion. But, why not track the amount of minutes the class writes over time instead to show just how much these daily goals add up? This idea was inspired by Ruth Ayres (2019), who, rather than record the number of words she wrote each day, added them up over the course of a month instead. Over that time, the daily number grew from 779 words to 8,615.

Start by charting the number of minutes spent writing in the classroom over the course of the week on a simple calendar, and watch the minutes grow over time—for example, Monday, 15 minutes; Tuesday, up to 31; and Wednesday, 47 minutes so far! See how this changes the focus to how the daily quotas add up over time? By setting expectations for the writerly lives we hope to have, we can build a writing life day by day and incrementally celebrate our success over time.

Try the 5 × 5 Method

Once you've gotten your notebook and found the time to write in it, the question becomes *What do I write?* There are many ways to uncover potential writing ideas, from heart maps (Heard 2016) and lists to picture prompts and sentence starters. I have tried each, but the 5 × 5 method is what really works for me.

The 5 × 5 method was inspired by a writing session with Charles R. Smith Jr., author of *I Am America*. The premise is simple: Start by listing five categories, such as favorite foods, pets, movies, and experiences. Then, list five detailed examples for each of those categories, but get specific. Don't list spaghetti as your favorite food; list grandma's spicy Italian spaghetti with fettuccine noodles instead. Figure 5.1 offers a glimpse of my own 5 × 5 notebook page.

Once the page is complete, you'll have twenty-five potential writing ideas that are sure to inspire the pages of your notebook. And if you vary your format, you'll have even more. You might write a small-moment memoir about cooking with your grandmother, a poem professing your love of fettuccine noodles, or a letter to your grandmother thanking her for the memories she has given you. The simplicity of the 5 × 5 grid not only generates many ideas for writing, it also launches you into a personal exploration of yourself.

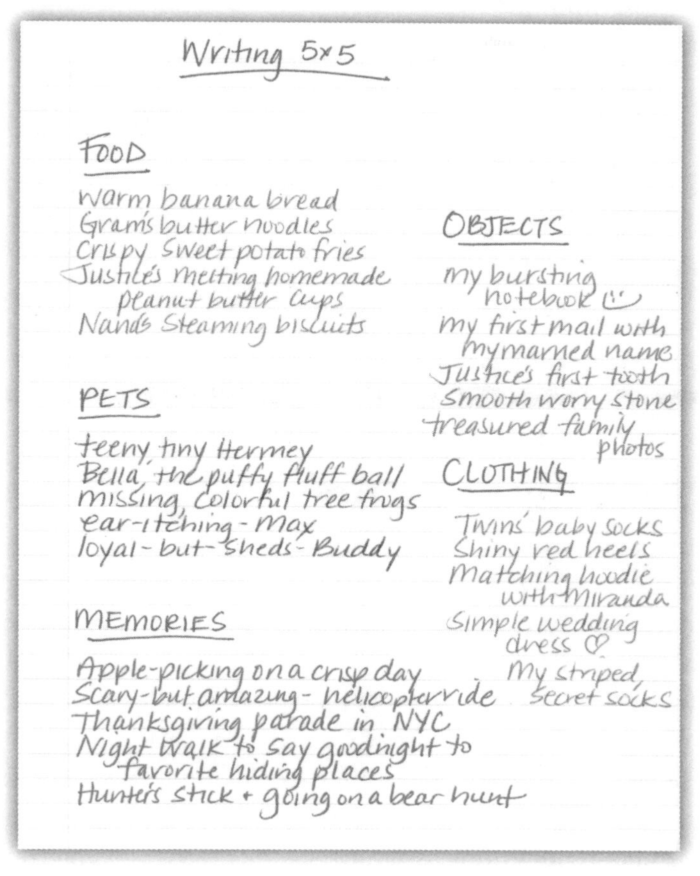

FIGURE 5.1 *A glimpse of my own 5 × 5 notebook page*

Here's How to Bring It to the Classroom

You can easily try the 5 × 5 method with your students to generate twenty-five possible writing topics that hold personal meaning for them. If you need to, you can modify your lists based on the age of your students. A 3 × 3 list would work better for some, and a 10 × 10 list would challenge others. Start the year by generating topics that help students get to know one another, and as the year progresses, you can offer a new set of topics each month. Figure 5.2 shows a list of possible 5 × 5 writing topics for brainstorming.

Possible Topics for 5 × 5 Brainstorming	
Foods	Pets
Locations	Ice cream
Movies	Friends
Songs	Family
Family members	Collections
Superheroes	

FIGURE 5.2 *Possible topics for 5 × 5 brainstorming*

Quiet Your Inner Critic

If I were to ask a group of educators if they were writers, I am certain that a good number of them would reply with a single word: no. Regardless of the fact that they write for functional reasons throughout their busy days, many define writing as something done for more creative and aspirational reasons. Unlike reading, where we define ourselves as readers simply because we *can* read, writing is perceived differently. Simply because we *can* write doesn't mean we *are* writers. Many of us seem to have an inner writing critic spouting myths about our abilities on a repeating loop that discourages us from reaching for a writing utensil. We may remember rigid writing assignments, the dreaded red pen, and even anxious moments of sharing our writing with others. I've heard that it takes five positive experiences to overcome a single negative one, but in my experience, it takes many more to quell our inner writing critics and listen to our writing dreams instead.

Declare #WhyIWrite

Since 2009, the National Day on Writing® celebrates writing each year on October 20th and has encouraged thousands of people to claim their voice as a writer, to write what matters most to each of them. Using the #WhyIWrite hashtag, the National Council of Teachers of English (NCTE) invites writers to share what compels each of them "to pick up a pen, sharpen a few pencils, dust off the chalk, find a marker that works, or tap your keyboard." Taking the time to think about why writing matters in our lives can go a long way in building a consistent writing habit.

Turn to a new page in your notebook, and label it #WhyIWrite at the top. Spend some time thinking about why writing calls to you, why you want to keep a writing notebook, and why writing matters in your life. You might create a list, write a narrative explanation, draw or sketch, or use any combination thereof. The important thing is that you spend time declaring why you write—and honor your writing identity.

Once your page is complete, you might declare your writing intentions alongside others in the #WhyIWrite initiative. Here are a few suggestions inspired by NCTE's (2020) website: try to write in a new genre—a letter, poem, blog; look through old pieces of writing or journals and pull out a section you'd like to share; explore a new medium—record a podcast, write an email, take a photograph to accompany a piece of writing, add a drawing or sketch to your writing; make a plan with your friends or family to write together.

Joining the #WhyIWrite initiative is a powerful way not only to publicly acknowledge yourself as a writer but also to connect with other writers brave enough to do the same.

Here's How to Bring It to the Classroom

#WhyIWrite is the perfect celebration to bring to your students. Celebrate #WhyIWrite any time of the year in your classroom by encouraging students to share the reasons they write both in school and at home. They can post their reasons on a graffiti wall, write them in chalk on the sidewalks leading up to the school, format them into hashtags to mimic social media posts, or create story bubbles provided by NCTE in its online toolkit (www.whyiwrite.us). You'll find an example of one student's #WhyIWrite declarations in Figure 5.3.

Provide long stretches of time for students to write and celebrate their writing with others through author shares or gallery walks. Take photos of the celebration and share them on the #WhyIWrite hashtag on social media, if you have permission. And if you can, bring your whole school into the celebration!

The National Day on Writing is a day to celebrate every writer, no matter how experienced, confident, creative, or accomplished we think we are. It is a way to publicly acknowledge the role that writing plays in our lives and to celebrate the writing potential patiently waiting inside each of us.

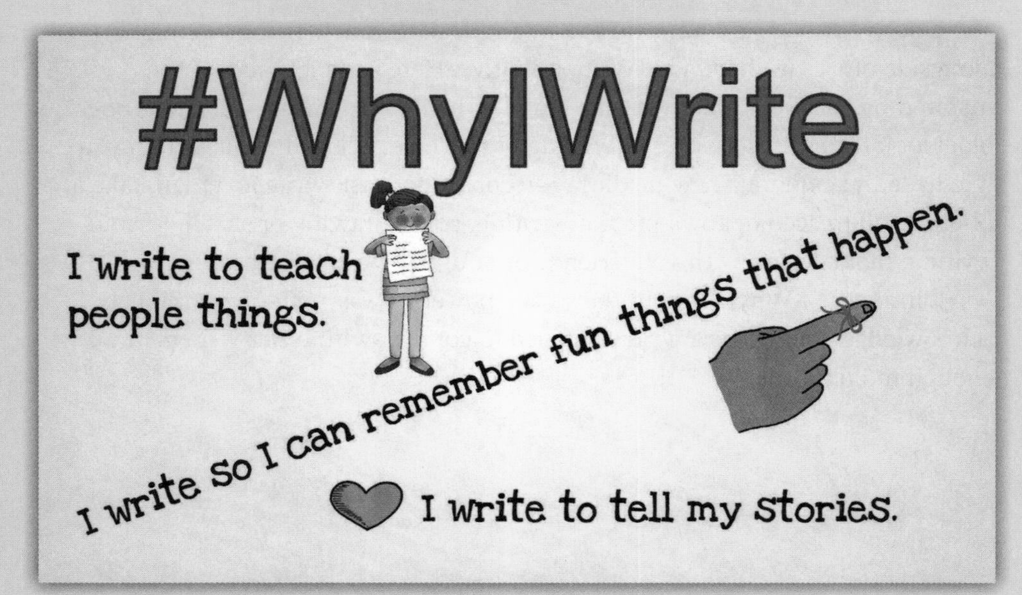

FIGURE 5.3 *A student's #WhyIWrite declarations*

Convert Challenges to Goals

Part of quieting our inner critic is to tackle the writing challenges we face in growing our writing lives and habits. Once we prove that inner critic wrong, we can better incorporate writing habits into our daily lives.

Turn to a clean page in your writer's notebook. List all the challenges you face in growing your writing life: finding the time to write, figuring out what to write about, letting go of perfectionism and experimenting with craft, getting over writer's block, wondering what others will think about your writing, feeling your writing is worthy enough, and more. Get all of your challenges and worries out of your head and onto the paper.

Now, grab a highlighter and highlight the items that you can actually do something about, such as finding the time to write or deciding what to write about. Let go of all the rest, including wondering what others will think. Look through your list of highlighted items and choose one. Now, put all your energy into that one thing and overcome the obstacles you face as a writer, one goal at a time. The next paragraph describes how.

Turn the page in your notebook and write your writing challenge at the top. Spend the next five minutes brainstorming what you might do to overcome that challenge. If you find you are done generating solutions before the timer stops, then keep brainstorming. You might be surprised at what you come up with when you let your mind continue to wander. Figure 5.4 tackles three common writing challenges as an example.

Now, when a writing obstacle emerges, flip to this page in your notebook and choose a strategy to overcome it. Each day you write strengthens your writing habit, and those successful days of writing string together over time to strengthen your writing identity. When you've successfully tackled your first writing challenge, you can move to the next one.

I don't have any time to write!	I am not sure what to write about!	I have writer's block!
Set your alarm five minutes earlier and spend those minutes writing in your notebook.	Create a list of people, places, and topics that matter to you in your notebook. Revisit the list when you need inspiration.	Abandon your need to write lengthy text. Create a list, or sketch your thinking instead.
Keep a notebook on your bedside table and jot down an observation about your day each night before heading to sleep.	Choose a word to write about or sketch. Sign up for the word of the day from Merriam-Webster or visit TeachWrite's Instagram account for a daily prompt (www.instagram.com/teachwriteedu).	Let go of your perfectionism and put something on the page. Only you decide who sees your writing, and not everything must be shared.
Purchase a small calendar, and challenge yourself to write one sentence a day in the daily spaces.	Scan the world around you. What observations could you make? What do you wonder about? What does it make you think of?	Go for a walk or simply change locations. Clear your head from the other items vying for your attention to allow for new ideas.
Schedule five to ten minutes of writing during your lunch break.	Scroll your camera roll. Browse through your saved pictures until you find one that sparks an idea.	Borrow inspiration from others. Browse a mentor text, or read the writing of others to elicit new thinking and ideas.
Carry your writer's notebook with you at all times as a visible reminder to add your thinking to the pages.	Google "creative writing prompts" and choose one to get started.	Do something creative. Sing a song, play with the kids, or get out your adult coloring book. This often leads to creative writing, too.
Create an alert on your phone reminding you to write.	Write anyway. Just start moving your pencil across the page and see what emerges. You can even begin with the words *I don't know what to write about.*	Don't stress or overthink it. Every writer experiences writer's block, and if you have it, it means you are a writer. Change your perspective and see what happens next.

FIGURE 5.4 *Three common writing challenges and possible solutions*

Here's How to Bring It to the Classroom

Once you take concrete steps to gain control of your writing life, you can help your students do the same. Let's face it. If we find it hard to find the time to write and stay focused and confident about our writing abilities as adults, then our students are probably facing the same obstacles. Try this. Give students a stack of colorful sticky notes and ask them to write each writing challenge or obstacle they face on an individual note. Post the sticky notes on a common wall so that the colorful opportunities to tackle our challenges are front and center. Gather the students around you and read the posted notes aloud. As you read, guide your students to see any patterns that are emerging, and start clustering the sticky notes together to represent broad challenges to tackle based on the needs of your class. Talk about the themes and patterns, and invite discussion.

Together, choose one challenge to tackle: one that meets the needs of the majority of students and is sure to have an impact on the classroom writing community. Turn the challenge into an "I can" statement such as this: *When I don't know what to write about, I can . . .*, or *When I am not sure how to spell a word, I can . . .* Together, list ways students could overcome that challenge. Here are some ways to tackle building writing stamina: track the number of minutes the class writes independently, create notes of inspiration on index cards to place on classmates' desks, find a writing partner for support, turn to a mentor text for ideas. You'll find an example in Figure 5.5.

Post the anchor charts where they are clearly visible for all and add picture icons if needed. Teach whole-class minilessons based on the challenges your students face, and form strategy groups for students needing additional support. Empower your students to take control of their writing lives just as you did your own.

When I don't know what to write about, I can......

→ Look at my heart map.

→ Think about my day.

→ Write about something I love.

→ Choose a topic from the writing jar.

→ Ask my writing partner for ideas.

FIGURE 5.5 *An "I can" chart to build writing stamina*

Start with a Sentence a Day

A sentence journal is exactly what it sounds like: a place to write one sentence each and every day to build a writing habit over time. That one sentence can be anything: a memorable event from the day, something you read that you do not want to forget, something that you are grateful for, something that makes you happy, and anything else on your mind. It is a sentence just for you to treasure—but all those sentences add up. Did you know if you wrote just one ten-word sentence a day for 365 days, you'd write 36,500 words over the course of the year. That's like writing a novella!

My first sentence journal was actually a small calendar with just enough space in the squares to hold a sentence, but the simple fact of putting pen to paper each and every day mattered. Sure, life was busy, but I could manage one sentence, right? And often that one sentence would lead to more writing. Not only that, I started paying more attention to what was happening in my life instead of hustling through my days so I could have something to write about. My sentence journal became a keystone habit, positively impacting other aspects of my life.

Vow to write one sentence a day in your notebook for one week. List the sentences down the page for as many days in a row as you can. Or, print out a monthly calendar to write in each day, and tuck it into the pages of your notebook. If you forget a day, don't get discouraged; just "show up" to the page on the next day. It's waiting patiently for you. Starting with just one sentence builds your writing habits and ultimately, your confidence, too.

Here's How to Bring It to the Classroom

I'll never forget the time I went for a winter walk with my three children when they were little. As we wandered through the woods, three large dogs barreled toward us with their owner holding the leashes and trailing behind. They came upon us, sniffed, licked, and jumped and then left as fast as they had arrived. When we arrived home, my then five-year-old ran inside to find his father, shouting, "Dad, Dad, guess what?" I thought the next words out of his mouth would be to tell the story of the dogs, but it wasn't. Instead he said, "I know what I'm going to write about in writer's workshop tomorrow!" He was so used to writing every day that he started looking at the world as a place full of writing inspiration, and your students can, too. Start the day with a few moments to write a sentence, or end the day with a bit of writing instead. If students need inspiration, try a bit of prompting:

- What went well today?
- What's one thing that you learned today?
- What makes you happy today?
- What are you grateful for?
- What do you want to remember today?

You might even introduce your students to a word-of-the-day routine to spark their daily sentence. Jen Laffin of TeachWrite offers teacher–writers a daily word to inspire a writing habit, and the same concept could work for students. Each day, project a word on the whiteboard or share an image for students to view. You can use the daily word of the day from TeachWrite as inspiration or check the word of the day from Merriam-Webster.

Adopt Writerly Practices

I love meeting my treasured authors in real life for a few reasons, but I especially love learning about their writing lives so I can adopt their writerly practices for my own writing. I devour articles, posts, and podcasts on what writers do so I, too, can live a life inspired by reading and writing. Here's some of what I've learned:

- Writers write every day. Sometimes this writing is connected to their current writing project and sometimes it is not.
- Writers push their writing boundaries. They strengthen their writing muscles with writing experiences, exercises, and creative endeavors.
- Writers experience the world around them. Writing needs inspiration, so living a writerly life means living life to the fullest—and taking note of it.
- Writers move. Changing writing locations can inspire different kinds of writing. Writers walk to clear their head and make room

for new ideas, to experience nature, and to simply change their scenery and creative energy.

- Writers read. They read wide and deep, taking note of the craft moves they might want to emulate—and they explore those options in their own writing.
- Writers embrace their uniqueness. We all have our own quirks that make us who we are, but writers and artists seem to better embrace those idiosyncrasies and use them to harness their creativity.
- Writers build support networks, such as writing partners and accountability groups.

I encourage you to embrace these writing practices, to learn from them, and, ideally, to try them on for size and make them your own. To explore more, you might listen to *The Writer Files,* Kelton Reid's podcast for studying the habits, habitats, and brains of renowned writers.

Design Your Studio for Positivity and Success

My friend Julie makes handcrafted jewelry inspired by nature and infused with symbolism. Her breathtaking designs evoke a deep connection to the natural world, and her studio is filled to the brim with natural materials, gemstones, supplies, and almost every jewelry-making tool you could think of. I love visiting her studio because it evokes a great feeling of possibility. Surrounded by the raw materials of her craft, she is able to create art. The same applies to writing. When we surround ourselves with writing tools and messages of positive possibilities, we can better settle into a writing routine.

Whether you have a large spacious room for writing, a small corner of the kitchen, or a portable tote bag full of supplies you carry with you, you can ensure that your space promotes successful, creative, and inspired writing with just a few steps:

1. Choose your writing space. This doesn't have to be a large space. Choose a corner of a room, a nook hidden away, a comfortable chair, or even a portable basket full of needed materials.
2. Gather your supplies. And no, not just any supplies will do. Give yourself permission to indulge in the supplies that speak to your

writing heart. For me, this means my notebook, my big box of colorful markers, and my beloved gel pens. Surround yourself with the writing tools that beg to be written with.

3. Now, add positivity. Surround your space with invitations to write and positive affirmations for writing. Tape inspirational quotes to the cover of your notebook. You'll find some of my favorites in Figure 5.6. Leave sticky notes of encouragement in your writing space. Print graphics and memes that invite you to write and that quell your inner critic—and insert them into picture frames to display. And when someone compliments your writing, write down their words of encouragement and post those, too.
4. Bring in nature if you can. I have a terrible green thumb, but even I can care for those small air plants and succulents—and they're small enough to brighten even the tiniest spaces.

Inspirational Quotes About Writing
"You might not write well every day, but you can always edit a bad page. You can't edit a blank page." —Jodi Picoult
"Start writing, no matter what. The water does not flow until the faucet is turned on." —Louis L'Amour
"Every secret of a writer's soul, every experience of his life, every quality of his mind, is written large in his works." —Virginia Woolf
"And by the way, everything in life is writable about if you have the outgoing guts to do it, and the imagination to improvise. The worst enemy to creativity is self-doubt." —Sylvia Plath
"Writing is really a way of thinking—not just feeling but thinking about things that are disparate, unresolved, mysterious, problematic or just sweet." —Toni Morrison

FIGURE 5.6 *A collection of inspirational quotes about writing*

5. Remove distractions. Keep your writing space clear of clutter. This way, you're not tempted to clean up, pay the bills, or start another task on your to-do list. Close unnecessary tabs on your computer, and silence your cell phone.

https://bit.ly/3eTdg5D

Scan to view pictures of writers' writing spaces

Now that you have carved out a dedicated writing space, you're more likely to visit and use it even if that means taking your portable bin out to the porch to write with the breeze. Are you wondering what the writing spaces of your beloved authors look like? You might enjoy reading *The Writer's Desk* by Jill Krementz (1996), a book that captures photos of famous writers' workspaces as inspiration for your own. For inspiration, you can also scan the QR code for pictures of more than a hundred writers' writing spaces.

Here's How to Bring It to the Classroom

We might not be able to create personalized writing studios for each student in our classroom, but we can create a shared writing studio with elements that appeal to all writers. Here are some possibilities to include in your classroom studio:

- A wide range of materials: Stock the writing studio with ample materials for students to choose from, such as different kinds of paper and writing utensils. These choices mattered in your own writing life and they can make a difference in students' writing lives as well.
- Writing tools: Ensure that the studio is stocked with the tools your writers will need to live a writerly life, such as sticky notes, highlighting tape, glue sticks, tape, and scissors.
- Mentor materials: Surround your students with mentor texts, anchor charts, demonstration pages, and microprogressions (Roberts and Beattie Roberts 2016) to support their efforts and set them up for independence.
- Notes of encouragement: Post the same inspirational quotes and affirmations in your students' writing studio as you did in your own. Switch out the quotes and graphics in the picture frames often to renew students' enthusiasm over time.

Invite your students to help design and create a writing studio that works best for them. By working together to gather and organize materials and to request new writing tools, students will have ownership in the space and make it their own.

You can also carve out smaller writing studios for individual students by creating portable writing studios. Provide each student with an empty cereal box, shoe box, or even a large manilla envelope to decorate and personalize. Stock the portable studios with students' supplies, notebook, and writing mentors, just as you might have your own. Students can reach for their portable studio to create a personalized writing haven right within the classroom.

Write Just Because

One of the things I admire about my favorite authors is their enthusiasm to write "just because." My task-oriented mindset prevented me from indulging in writing for no apparent reason at all, and it took a long while for me to realize that writing exploration—tinkering and writing "just because"—actually strengthens writing overall. Taking time to play with writing, to be still with my thoughts, and to just explore what I am capable of does wonders for my sense of self-worth as well as my writing identity.

Your writer's notebook is the perfect place to explore these possibilities and strengthen writing muscles you might not have known you possessed. Here are a few of my favorite ways to build my writing muscles:

- Adopt a Seinfeld mentality and write about absolutely nothing for five minutes or more without stopping. Just start with one sentence and move onto the next. The sentences might be disconnected, outlandish, mundane, or magnificent; the important thing is that your writing utensil is moving— and you'll see where it takes you.
- Go for a walk and snap pictures of what intrigues you: something in nature, a building, a person, an object. Choose one and describe it by listing as many words as possible. Turn your list into a poem or imagine it as a central aspect of your next writing piece.

- Doodle. A fellow literacy coach introduced me to *The Art of Doodle Words* by Sarah Alberto (2018) to strengthen my creative muscles. I love choosing a word to turn into a creative doodle in my notebook, often jump-starting a longer writing piece. Check out her YouTube channel *Doodles by Sarah* for oodles of inspiration.
- Write a story completely in text messages or emoticons. You might be surprised how much thinking and craft is needed to pull this off—and it's a lot of fun, too!
- Eavesdrop. Yes, eavesdrop. Gather snatches of talk (Fletcher 1996) you hear throughout the day and capture them in your notebook. Choose one and imagine a scenario around it.
- Write in response to a creative prompt. I love taking out Colby Sharp's *The Creativity Project* (2018) and choosing a prompt from my favorite authors to try for myself.

Here's How to Bring It to the Classroom

Ralph Fletcher (2017) celebrates "greenbelt writing": writing that is raw, unmanicured, uncurated (39). This low-stakes, playful, and even wild writing sparks students to write, engages their imagination, and ensures that they experience the pleasures of writing. Imagine if we had all learned just how important this greenbelt writing was to our writing lives at an early age. You can invite greenbelt writing into your classroom by providing students with daily time to freely write in their writer's notebook, posting "just because" writing prompts to get students' creativity flowing, and encouraging students to become inspired by their peers.

Take your cue from Marcia Golub (1999) and create a collection of writing exercises for your students, either collected or invented. Put each writing exercise on a slip of paper (or perhaps on a digital slide) and slip it into a decorated envelope or jar created just for this purpose. When students have difficulty getting started or feel they have nothing to write about, encourage them to randomly choose a writing exercise to try. The novelty of the prompts may be just the thing they need to get out of a writing rut and into new writing territory. Here are a few prompts to help you get started:

- You're sitting on your bed and suddenly, a note is slipped under your door. Open it. What does it say?
- Choose a favorite song. Why does it matter to you?
- If you were given a magic wand, what would you wish for?
- Write an acrostic poem for this date in time. Write the day vertically down the page (e.g., Wednesday) and add an event from the day to represent each letter.
- Look out the window. List every object you see. Choose one and create a poem.
- Think of a friend or family member you have not seen in a while. Write a letter, email, or text message to that person.
- Ask your writing partner to think of five words. Create a story using those five words.

Use the envelope or jar as a launching point for greenbelt writing, but remember, this kind of writing is not for evaluation or grading—it is for building a writing habit that leads to a strong writing identity.

Practice the Art of Noticing

As busy educators, we have a lot on our plates. We juggle competing responsibilities at school and home and often multitask our way through the day. While this multitasking can be effective in the short term, I've found it wreaks havoc on long-term well-being. As Rob Walker, the author of *The Art of Noticing* (2019) reminds us, "A hypereffective schedule designed to maximize productivity is, in fact, more likely to distract you from what's important than help you discover it" (xiv). Writers pay attention to the world around them and have perfected the art of noticing. They find the extraordinary in the ordinary.

Let's take Walker's (2019) advice and devote one hour a week (to start!) to becoming more present in the moment—to notice the world around us and become more curious within it. Here are four of my favorite prompts from Walker's (2019) book to jump-start your noticing:

- Spend five minutes looking out of a window you typically ignore. Find three things you've never seen from that perspective. Write about them.
- Take a color walk. Notice the colors around you and how they make you feel. How do colors play out across your day and impact how you see the world?
- Change your location. We are creatures of habit. We frequent the same stores, sit in the same seats, take the same commute. So, change it up! And really pay attention to the new perspectives you find.
- Pay attention like a child. We often find ourselves surrounded by the familiar, but what might a child say about these familiar surroundings? How can you perceive them in a new way?

This kind of slowing down and noticing is sure to inspire our writing as well as our lives. Walker (2019) notes that "anybody interested in thinking creatively seeks (needs) to notice what has been overlooked or ignored by others, to get beyond distractions and attend to the world" (xi). When we do, we don't just see things differently, we actually *see* things that we often overlook in the busyness of our everyday lives. And once we see them, we must allow ourselves the time to truly pay attention and notice them, to become enchanted with them, and to document them so they are not easily forgotten. These noticings are ideal material for our writer's notebooks. Sometimes, I simply note what I see in my notebook. Other times, I snap pictures of those noticings to tape into my notebook or scroll through on my phone.

Here's How to Bring It to the Classroom

Our students are naturally more tuned into the world around them, noticing things adults easily miss. We can harness this attention and curiosity about the world to boost students' writing. Encourage students to truly notice the world around them and use those noticings to boost their writing. Here are some ideas to share with them:

- Choose an object and study it. Use the five senses to describe it.
- Take a walk. Sketch an interesting view and write a story about it.
- Listen to the conversation around you. Turn it into a series of text messages.
- Find something unexpected. Imagine how it arrived there and tell a story from the perspective of the object.

When we develop a habit of noticing, we develop our connections with the world around us, uncovering what was once hidden to our eyes and to the page. By making a conscious effort to become more fully present, to really observe, notice, and become more curious about the world around us, we can cultivate a more robust writing life and create a beautiful legacy of living on the page.

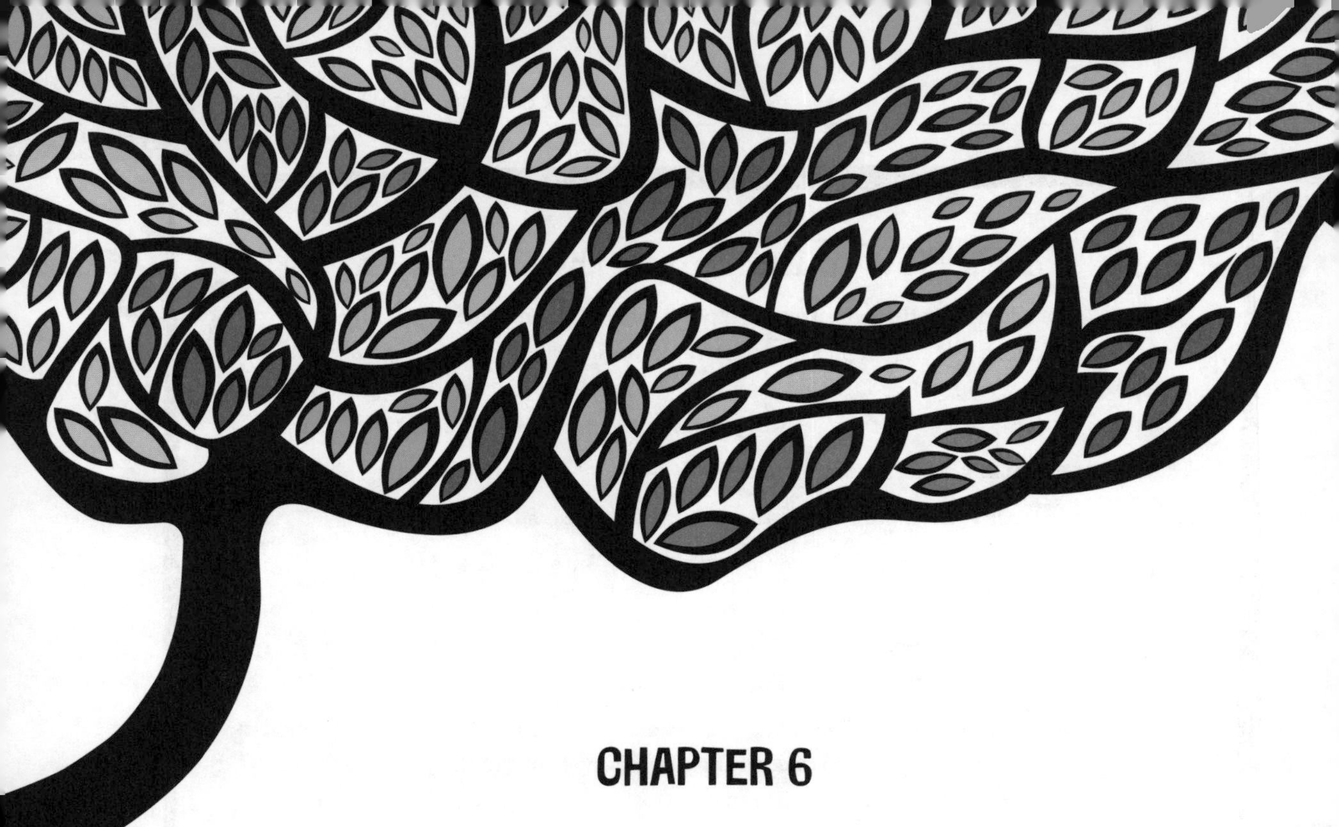

CHAPTER 6

Honor Our Writing Hearts

My feelings toward writing over the course of my life look a bit like an electrocardiogram (EKG). I adored writing in my childhood when I could write to dream, think, and make sense of my changing world. In high school, however, my thoughts toward writing shifted and changed as the demands grew larger and the restrictions grew tighter. College initially brought renewed pleasure to my writing life as I explored new genres and writing styles. I enjoyed lesson planning and keeping reflective journals about my teaching and learning. But as I continued my studies, I became less enchanted with case-study reports and formal academic genres. It wasn't until I started blogging that I finally found the kind of writing that set my heart on fire: narrative nonfiction. I love writing articles and blog posts that invite readers into the content, renew their own sense of curiosity and learning, and provide nuggets of ideas, resources, and inspiration to support their teaching minds and hearts.

Write to Explore Your Sense of Self

As adults, we typically choose to engage in things that make us feel productive, happy, and content. We typically do not engage in activities that we do not enjoy, do not help us feel better about ourselves, or serve no larger purpose in our lives. And this includes writing. When writing feels like something outside ourselves, we do not privilege it in our lives—but when it helps us to make sense of ourselves, we feel the need for it.

Honor the Commonplace

Merriam-Webster (2020b) defines *commonplace* as "commonly found or seen: ordinary, unremarkable." Our lives are full of the commonplace: the gadgets in our kitchen, the clutter in the living room, our morning habits to start the day, where we store our coats and bags, and our mealtime rituals and routines, to name a few. Commonplace books collect the ordinary routines of our lives and are dated all the way back to the Roman and Greek philosophers who documented their thoughts, daily meditations, and important quotes.

Over time, the commonplace book grew to include any kind of knowledge and information from a particular time period: recipes, letters, formulas, prices, prayers, etc. And that can turn the mundane into magic. When we consciously bring the commonplace to our attention, it can tell us a great deal about who we are and how we live our life. Exploring the commonplace that surrounds us, pondering it, questioning it, and, ultimately, celebrating it, provides us with opportunities to explore our sense of self through writing. Here are some ways to capture the simple, everyday routines of life through writing, those everyday moments we typically fail to notice the significance of but miss deeply when they are gone. Turn to a fresh page in your notebook for each of these ideas:

- Document your space. Head to a room in your house, and snap a few pictures to add to your notebook. If you can't print the images, sketch the room instead. Then, write about what you see. Why is the coffeepot where it is? Why is the stack of books next to your bed significant? What does the dented dining room table remind you of? You might list your thoughts, write them as a narrative, or even get creative with a bit of poetry.

- Document your day. Choose a day to document your life. Don't wait for the weekend when something "good" might happen; choose a regular day of the week full of the commonplace. List the activities that make up your day and snap pictures of them if you can. Later on, reflect. Jot your thinking, capture quotes from the day, share the significance of each tiny event.
- Document the world. Date your notebook page, and list everything currently going on in the world around you, from the community events and the sale at the bakery to celebrated holidays and major world events. Add your thoughts about each event and why it matters to you at that moment. If you'd like, tape event clippings to the pages for added documentation.

Storytelling our lives in this way gives us a personal outlet for writing and provides opportunities to learn more about ourselves. What's the story behind why you have the morning routine you have? What's the story behind your lunch box and how you pack it? What's the story behind how you fold the laundry and where you stack it? These commonplace stories make up the fabric of our lives and are ripe for exploring. Documenting our rituals and routines helps us think more carefully about who we are, what we value, and how we live our lives.

Here's How to Bring It to the Classroom

We can expand this commonplace collecting to our classrooms to tell the story of learning throughout the year. You might dedicate a separate notebook as a commonplace book to archive the stories of your classroom. Capture your classroom spaces, the lived routines, and the artifacts of learning. What stories do they tell? Katie Keier, coauthor of *Catching Readers Before They Fall* (Johnson and Keier 2010) uses a linear calendar to capture the learning in her classroom. She purchases a yearly calendar and separates it, displaying each month horizontally across a classroom wall. Each month, the class interacts with the calendar just as we might interact with our own: planning for the week, noting important events, and recording activities. At the end of the month, she brings the class together for a reflective discussion on all they have experienced or accomplished. They write an interactive writing piece together and display it on the calendar wall along with pictures that document learning. This linear

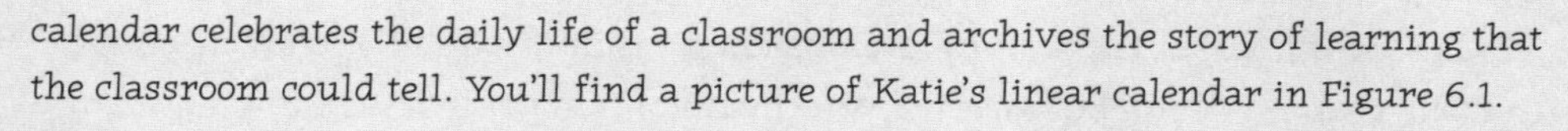
calendar celebrates the daily life of a classroom and archives the story of learning that the classroom could tell. You'll find a picture of Katie's linear calendar in Figure 6.1.

FIGURE 6.1 *Katie Keier's kindergarten linear calendar*

Uncover Your Writing Dreams

As a child, I had grand dreams. I was going to grow up to be a famous singer (Debbie Gibson, to be exact), an Olympic figure skater, and a world-famous cake decorator. Over time, those grand dreams were tucked further and further into my heart, buried under the business of growing older with new responsibilities, the reality of what can actually be accomplished, and, unfortunately, a whole lot of self-doubt. It wasn't until I was older and renewed my commitment to journaling and self-reflection that I once again uncovered those dreams. Now, I will still never be a famous singer, Olympic skater, or world-renowned cake decorator, but

I can sing with my children, brighten the long winter months on a frozen pond, and create the most delicious vanilla bean cupcakes you've ever tasted.

Let's think about the writing dreams deep inside you. Did you always hope to write that children's book? Have you dreamed of writing letters to your growing children to leave as your personal legacy to them? Or, have you wished for the time to pull all of your family recipes together and create a treasured cookbook? Turn to a fresh page in your writer's notebook and capture your writing dreams. Then, choose one big dream that matters most to you, and brainstorm small actions needed to get you closer to it. Figure 6.2 offers a few examples.

Think Big	Plan Small
Write a children's book.	• Research literary agents. • Draft a story line. • Find a mentor. • Join a writing group. • Take a creative writing course.
Create a family cookbook.	• Write a letter to family members requesting recipes. • Gather favorite recipes of your own. • Borrow multiple cookbooks from the library to serve as mentor texts. • Scour your favorite recipe sites to learn about the craft of writing a cookbook.
Launch a successful blog.	• Follow blogs that you admire. Pay close attention to why those sites capture your attention. • Find successful bloggers and ask for advice. • Write a draft of a few blog pieces to launch your content. • Sketch a possible logo and brand.
Write a grant to support your teaching.	• Take a workshop on successful grant writing. • Draft sections of your grant proposal and ask a trusted friend for feedback. • Boost your writing skills and learn about the ins and outs of grant writing.

FIGURE 6.2 *Steps to reaching writing dreams*

You might have noticed that many of these goals involve actual writing, but they also involve living as writers in multiple ways: observing, learning, talking with others, reading like a writer, expanding your writing skills, asking for feedback. These are all writerly habits that support reaching our writing dreams.

Scroll through your personal list and choose one small action you could take today. Moving forward, dedicate at least fifteen minutes a day for the next week to getting yourself closer to your writing dream. By taking just fifteen minutes to engage in writerly habits that support the writing that lives deep in our hearts, we bring ourselves closer to our writing dreams and realize they are within reach.

Here's How to Bring It to the Classroom

What if we took this same approach with students in the classroom? Carve out time to ask students about their dreams, especially their writing dreams. Be prepared to give examples as students will likely need support for dreaming outside of what writing looks like within school walls: writing a book, creating a family scrapbook, writing a video game manual, creating a website, and more. You'll find an example of one student's writing dreams and a page from her notebook in Figure 6.3.

“You change the world by being yourself.” Yoko Ono

FIGURE 6.3 *Pages from a student's quote book*

“I don't think of all the misery, but of the beauty that still remains.”

-Anne Frank-

Once you have learned more about your students' dreams as writers, think about how you could honor those dreams within the school day. Now, I'm not suggesting you abandon your writing standards or your school's writing curriculum, but I am suggesting you find ways to help make connections from them to what students personally hope to accomplish. I take my cue here from Cornelius Minor (2018), who urges teachers to make the curriculum personal and relevant for the students in front of them. Here's an example: If students are studying personal narrative, you can explain how learning about this can help those who are dreaming of writing their own book to share with the world. If students are studying word choice, you can show them how to transfer this skill to other writing, such as the video game handbook they are working on during free time. If we help students connect their writing in the classroom to their own writing dreams, we will ensure that students become more invested and engaged.

Write from the Soul

Many writing curriculums and units of study begin with an exploration of personal narrative writing because it allows students to write about what they are experts on: themselves. Adults often find this genre of writing a good entry point for their own writing lives for the same reason: you cannot get it wrong. Janet Connor (2009), author of *Writing Down Your Soul: How to Activate and Listen to the Extraordinary Voice Within*, describes soul writing as writing that focuses your attention squarely on the wisdom within you, pouring your soul onto the paper to ultimately change your life. Connor adds that when you engage in big conversations with yourself on the page, you might find yourself contemplating ideas you've never considered, saying things you've never said, asking questions you've never asked. And once you start writing, your words lead to more ideas, intuition, inspiration, wisdom, opportunities, challenges, and more questions (9). I agree. Soul writing doesn't just help us build a writerly life, it helps us live it more fully. If we show up to the page, write freely about what is on our minds and hearts, and listen to where the pen might take us, we can learn much about life and living in the process.

According to Connor (2009), there are essentially four steps to soul writing: show up, open up, listen up, and follow up. Notice how this places the focus on what writing can do for our soul, rather than on what the writing looks like on the page. Let's try it.

Show up and open up by turning to a fresh page in your notebook, or if you're like me, you might write in a separate notebook hidden away for safekeeping. Others might feel more comfortable writing on a device, the file saved safely under a name only they can decode. Just start writing based on the events in your life and the emotions you feel in the moment, whatever they may be. Take a few breaths and start writing in a stream of consciousness without worrying about the content or form of what is appearing on the page. If you need a few ideas, here are a few prompts to get you started:

- What are your current feelings and emotions?
- What brings you joy and happiness?
- What are your worries, fears, and stressors?
- What are your dreams, goals, and aspirations?

Then, listen up and follow up. If you truly wrote in a stream of consciousness without focusing on form, then you likely captured a great deal of thought on the page. Pause for a moment after writing and read what you've written. A few things might happen. First, you might be shocked at what you find. When we let go of expectations and conventions and simply write what we feel, we often write far more than expected. Second, you might uncover things you didn't know about yourself or your current situation. Third, you might realize the power your writing holds to heal from within. When we write from the soul, our soul writes back.

Here's How to Bring It to the Classroom

The school day dictates the content students learn and the kind of reading and writing students engage in. While this might work for some students, it doesn't for others and they may feel disconnected from their learning. Provide outlets for students to write from their own personal experiences to learn more about themselves. Here are some prompts that might help students write from the heart:

- My favorite things about my life right now are . . .
- If I could change one thing, I would change . . .
- If I had three wishes, I would wish for . . .

- Here are ten things that make me smile: . . .
- I can't stop thinking about . . .
- If I could do anything, I would . . .
- If I could be anyone, I would . , .

Keep in mind that not all students prefer traditional forms of writing. Invite students to experiment with writing, drawing, sketchnoting, and other less traditional ways of bringing meaning to the page with varied writing utensils and mediums. Figure 6.4 shows fifth-grade student Ila Fisher's sketchnote about ten things that make her smile.

This kind of writing can become a creative outlet for some students and can change the way they view writing in their lives.

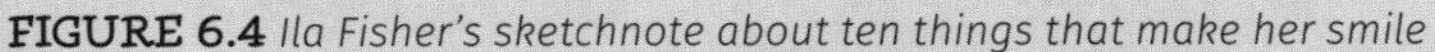
FIGURE 6.4 *Ila Fisher's sketchnote about ten things that make her smile*

Write to Explore Your Creativity

When we are young, creative play makes up the fabric of our days and for good reason. Play offers children opportunities to learn about the world, supports emotional regulation, and develops creativity (Mraz, Porcelli, and Tyler 2016). Boxes and blankets become castles. Empty paper-towel rolls become binoculars and kaleidoscopes. Stuffed animals come alive at tea parties and bedroom concerts. But as we grow, this kind of unstructured, imaginary play is slowly replaced with structured activities. When was the last time you played? I mean, really played. Can you remember the last time you did something simply for the sheer joy it brought you? Or the last time you put your device down and were entranced with the objects of the world rather than the screen? If you can, congratulations. But if you can't, you're not alone. The good news? We can do something about that.

Anne Lamott (1994) believes that a more inspired life full of restorative practices, play, and, yes, writing impacts our well-being. I especially love her view on writer's block or a lack of energy for writing. She posits that what we are feeling is not actually writer's block at all—it's a feeling of emptiness instead. According to Lamott, we simply need to do something that recharges, refreshes, and inspires because a life well-lived brings newfound energy and inspiration to the page.

Give Sketchnoting a Try

Sketchnoting is a form of creative note-taking that uses text, images, font, and color to represent thinking unique to each learner. So, rather than take notes in bulleted lists, sketchnoters might create a list but also add icons and images to boost memory and use colors to enhance understanding and tone. Sketchnoting helps personalize learning, appeals to both sides of the brain, helps retain information, increases focus, boosts creative thinking, makes connections across learning, helps us see the bigger picture, is calming and, quite frankly, is just plain fun (Duckworth 2020; McGregor 2019). If sketchnoting is new to you, I highly recommend that you listen to Tanny McGregor's Heinemann podcast episode on sketchnoting. To listen, scan the QR code.

https://bit.ly/3qsNZE3

Scan to listen to Tanny McGregor's podcast on sketchnoting

In sketchnoting, the sketchers are in control of how they represent thinking and learning, personalizing their work to meet their unique strengths and needs as learners. Each choice we make about color, lettering, size, orientation, and image holds personal meaning that ignites thinking and creativity. But I've learned not to overthink it. To see how this works, grab some color pencils or colorful markers, and follow these three easy steps for sketchnoting your name:

1. First, choose colors that match your personality, and write your name in a font that represents who you are. Is the font light and whimsical? Is it solid with bold lines? You decide.
2. Next, add words, phrases, and icons that capture who you are. Are you kind? Boisterous? Serious? Funny? Strive to think of ten ideas to add in either word or icon form. Check out The Noun Project (www.thenounproject.com) for over two million icon possibilities to borrow!
3. Finalize your piece by adding boxes and borders around your page. Draw a thick square border, play around with scalloped edges, or create a pattern of shapes instead.

There you have it! You successfully sketchnoted your name in three easy steps. Now, it's time to sketchnote something you might have written. Scroll through your notebook, and stop at a page where you have written a considerable portion of text. Or, think of something that captured your attention on social media or a recent blog post or article. Work through the same three steps you took to sketchnote your name, but sketchnote your thinking instead:

1. Choose colors to write with that match the theme or mood of your piece. Choose a font that captures the essence of the content and vary it throughout.
2. Next, write words, phrases, and text to document your understanding. Add icons to match and to make particular items stand out on the page. Use arrows and directional signals to organize your thinking.
3. Finalize your piece by adding boxes and borders around the content and page. This helps to organize your thinking even more so you can remember the content in a way that works best for you.

You'll likely need practice to feel comfortable with this kind of writing. I also recommend browsing Sylvia Duckworth's Flickr channel and Tanny McGregor's personal website for inspiring sketchnote possibilities. Just remember: a sketchnote is not meant to be perfect. It is a representation of thinking, process, and learning—something that is messy, complicated, and real. So don't be afraid to give it a try and see how your more creative side responds.

Here's How to Bring It to the Classroom

While adults might be hesitant to explore this kind of creative writing, our students typically are not. In my experience, students find sketchnoting to be a natural extension of the way they think, and they are very willing to capture their thinking and writing in this format. How can you bring sketchnoting to your students? Take a look at Sylvia Duckworth's (2018) sketchnote titled "5 Ways to Develop a Doodling Culture in Class" in Figure 6.5.

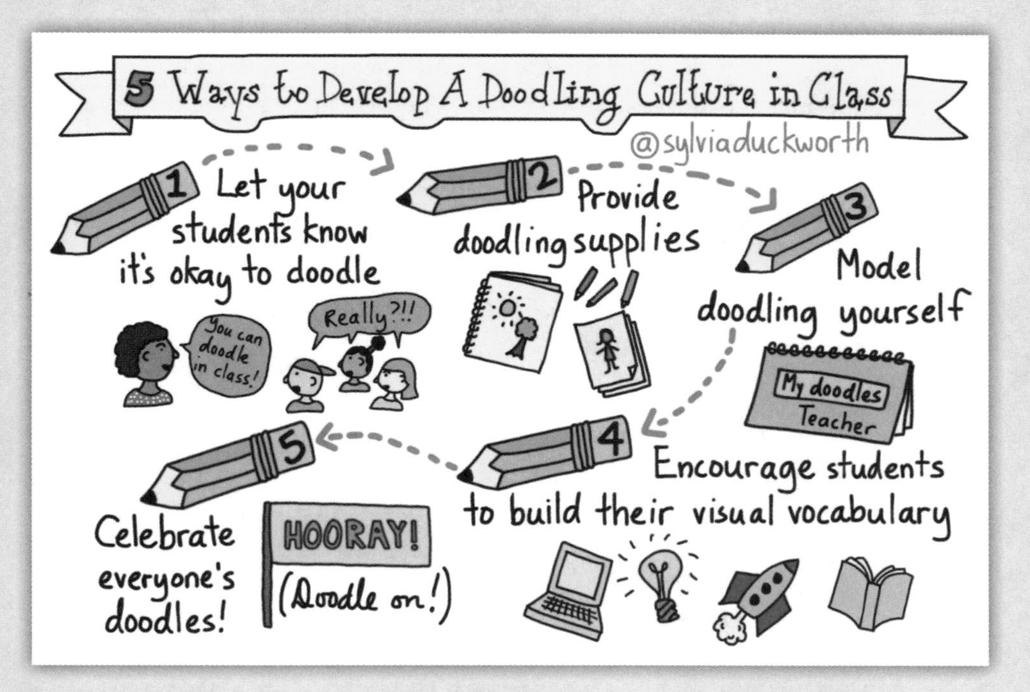

FIGURE 6.5 *Sylvia Duckworth's sketchnote on how to develop a doodling culture*

Then, get specific. Invite students to sketchnote a response to reading rather than write a response in text form only. Demonstrate how to take notes using sketchnotes to help personalize note-taking and boost memory. Encourage students to sketchnote

their thinking as a way to brainstorm their next writing piece. Challenge students to rewrite a page in their notebook in sketchnote form. When we give students (and ourselves) permission to tap into our more creative side, we might be surprised by what we can actually accomplish. Gone are the days of using only text to get the job done. Instead, indulge in sketchnoting to savor the process and to fuel your writing heart.

Layer Your Pages

When keeping a writer's notebook is new, it feels very much like a two-dimensional activity because only two materials are needed: your notebook and your writing utensil. While we might get creative with what we *do* with that writing utensil on those pages, chances are that it stays two-dimensional. This is a good place to start but not to end. When we layer different media and mediums onto our pages, we also layer our perspectives. Not only does the page become three-dimensional, our thinking does, too.

You can get started with a few easy suggestions to add more dimensional life to your pages:

- Add stickers: Accent your pages with stickers that complement your topic, theme, or mood.
- Layer photographs: Capture your heart in photographs, and use them to spark writing. You might even purchase a miniature photo printer or polaroid camera for this very purpose.
- Include pieces of text: Print poetry, copy a page of your book, or gather song lyrics to respond to on the page.
- Add book covers: Capture your responses to reading and include a small image of the book cover to bring a new layer of media to your page.
- Clip social-media sparks: Do you see something on social media that made you think? Don't just write about it; print out the post and include it on the page. Then react.

- Create a collage: Use magazines, newspapers, and other printed materials around the house to create a vision board, a possible scene, or a simple collection of items that sparked your thinking.
- Get scrappy: Browse the aisle of your local craft store for scrapbooking supplies you might use in your notebook. Think puffy stickers, borders and frames, background papers. Use materials like these to enhance your writing on the page.
- Include mementos: Gather your ticket stubs, receipts from treasured vacation dinners, leaves collected on a family walk, and more. You might tape an envelope or library pocket to the page to keep the items safely inside—and then write about the story they tell.

Layering media onto our page adds a level of thinking and reflection not quite possible without it. What materials do you choose and why do you choose them? What colors and themes complement your stories and why do they matter? How did you organize your materials on the page to represent the thinking in your head? And while this kind of creative notebooking and writing might take more time, it can have a tremendous impact on your thoughtful and creative writing abilities.

Here's How to Bring It to the Classroom

One simple way to make a connection to the classroom is to create collections of materials to inspire students to layer materials onto their notebook pages: stickers, tagboard, buttons, popsicle sticks, beads, images, letter tiles, and more. Gather and house containers full of crafty materials in the writing center or near an open table where students can browse and explore. Encourage students to experiment with the objects to enhance their notebook pages and deepen their level of thinking and creativity.

Then, just as you might have, encourage students to add stickers, photographs, clippings, and classroom mementos to their own writing pages as well. Their pages will likely be a treasured collection of personal growth and learning to celebrate their writing lives.

Write from Social Media Sparks

When we hear the word *sparks* in education, we might think of opening moves, hooks, and provocations to spark attention, motivation, or engagement. That is exactly the kind of spark that I am referring to here: tidbits of information that inspire writing on the page. Social media sparks are tweets, posts, blogs, podcasts, or other media from your feed that spark your thinking, tug at your heartstrings, or make you question how the world works. Since we personally curate our feed with people and organizations that matter most to us, our feed is ripe for writing about. Try this:

1. Head to your preferred social media feed and spend a minute or two browsing with the intention of finding something to spark writing in your notebook.
2. Stop when you find something that makes you react. Why is it speaking to you? What's compelling about it? What emotions does it evoke?
3. Turn to a fresh page in your notebook and start writing. Write a narrative response, create a list, sketch your emotions, recall a memory, refute information, and otherwise put your reaction on the page.
4. If you can, print out the spark and add it to the page. Or, label your page with pertinent information about the post that inspired it.

Just as we read mentor texts with a writer's eye, we can scroll our social media feeds with the same perspective. What's happening in the world that begs writing? What are your family and friends posting that you can connect with? I admit that I can become lost in scrolling, losing myself in my feeds if I'm not careful. But scrolling my feed with a writer's eye, instead of engaging in mindless scrolling that steals precious minutes from my day, changes the whole landscape for social media.

Here's How to Bring It to the Classroom

While we cannot set our students up with social media accounts, we *can* bring the world to them in a safe, developmentally appropriate way through online media. Here are a few options:

- Highlight current events in the world through student-friendly Internet sites, such as Time for Kids or Newsela. Project the texts for the whole class to experience, and engage in shared reading together, using the experience to launch personal writing.
- Appeal to students' curiosities and wonders. Display the Wonder of the Day from Wonderopolis and encourage students to write their own responses to the daily questions. They can even come up with their own and submit them to the site.
- Play a video clip. Sites like Great Big Story and The Kid Should See This offer short, powerful video clips sure to ignite thinking. My favorite? The "Bite into a Pickle Sandwich" video from Great Big Story about the sandwich shop in New Jersey making sandwiches without bread!

Things
I didn't know i'd miss in quarantine.
- toilet paper
- hand sanitizer (the good smelling ones)
- attending school
- the mall
- going to the grocery store (its the new vacation)
- breathing without a mask
- playing sports
- not being 6 feet apart.

FIGURE 6.6 *A student's response to an image depicting a toilet-paper shortage during COVID-19*

- Post a daily picture. The *New York Times*, *National Geographic*, NASA, and more offer daily and weekly pictures for viewers. You can use these websites to find appropriate images to spark your students' learning and writing. I like heading to Pixabay to search for my own copyright-free images to share with students as well. In Figure 6.6, you'll find a student's response to an image depicting a toilet-paper shortage during COVID-19.

These are all school-friendly ideas to bring the world to your students to spark writing, but depending on the grade level you teach, your students might even have their own social media feeds, as well. Encourage the students to read their feeds with a writer's eye and to share interesting posts with you that might be appropriate, and appealing, for the entire class.

Write to Explore Your Craft

I am a quote collector and one of my favorite quotes written on a sticky note adhered to my office wall is from Oprah Winfrey (2002): "A mentor is someone who allows you to see the hope inside yourself." I adore this definition of mentorship because it embodies the true importance of a mentor, which is *not* to demonstrate a skill or teach you content *nor* to show you finished products or even coach you to new levels of learning. The true role of a mentor is to help you see what is possible within yourself. Writing mentors, whether human or text, spark new possibilities for our own writing.

Mine for Writing Gems

I used to think that only published writers had writing craft that made their writing so powerful: the beautiful language, the carefully structured sentence, artful organization, and more. Craft moves were something that *actual* writers possessed, those that chose writing as their career, certainly not someone like myself whose writing was tucked away in a journal or in a computer file. But we all have our own writing craft that makes us unique. This writing craft can come in all shapes and forms: clever text messages, engaging emails, innovative lesson planning, personal journaling, creative crafting, report writing, published literature, and more. Each genre of our writing lives, even a functional one, has craft moves that enhance our purpose and message for our readers. And each one of us has particular strengths that make our writing unique. Katherine Bomer (2010) urges us to find the brilliance in every student's writing and name what we see so that it motivates our student writers. I believe that teachers need to do the same for themselves.

Take the next few minutes to clearly acknowledge your strengths as a writer. Write them down on a page in your notebook and flag it so you can return to it often. Here are some guiding questions to get you started:

- What kinds of writing do you feel good about? Why? Those are clues to your strengths. Do you have a knack for writing succinct emails? Or do you make others laugh with your text messages and note passing in meetings? Is your strength lesson planning, writing progress reports that show off students strengths? Are you a master list-maker? Or do you love creative writing in your journal? No matter what the genre or function, give yourself the gift of appreciation and let your strengths as a writer fill the page.
- Do others comment on your writing? If so, what do they say? Do your colleagues admire your ability to title a bulletin board or ask how you packed so much content into a 280-character tweet? Do your friends comment on your heartfelt posts and ability to really connect through personal social-media channels? Do others comment on your ability to wordsmith and choose the perfect adjective? Write those down, too.
- Look back at some of your notebook entries. What do you notice? Do you shine at writing about small moments in time, or are descriptive observations more your style? Are you adept at revising your pieces and open to flexible thinking? Do you have a knack for creative sketching and drawing?
- Finally, ask a trusted colleague or friend. This takes a bit of bravery, but you might share a few pieces of your writing with others and ask for feedback.

Take a minute to read over your list. Celebrate! So often we focus on what we believe we cannot do as writers instead of listing the many things we can. And this shift can change our entire perspective of writing and what we are capable of, something our students deserve as well.

Here's How to Bring It to the Classroom

Follow Bomer's (2010) suggestions for finding the hidden gems in your students' writing, too.

1. First, read your students' writing outside of your writing instruction or writing conferences so that you have the time to read it thoroughly. Reread each student's words as you would a difficult poem or text, expecting to find sense and meaning, even if difficult to find at first.
2. Point out what you feel the writer has done well and keep running notes on what you're noticing. Be descriptive. Avoid rubric-like jargon, such as *organized* and *detailed*, and use rich adjectives instead. Mark these gems with sticky notes to make them stand out.
3. Describe what you think the writer is doing in those places. Notice and name those craft moves, if you can. Keep track of what the student is exploring in the writing.
4. Think about the qualities of writing you've been studying as a class and decide on a teaching point that could nudge the writer forward. Take notes on where the student might need additional support to grow.
5. Note spelling, grammar, and punctuation concerns you must be mindful of, but don't let that lead your perspective as you view the writing.

With time and practice, mining students' writing (and our own!) for the beauty and brilliance within becomes second nature, and students can follow our lead to do the same for themselves. Give students a sticky note to read their writing pieces with a supportive eye and to note at least one thing they are proud of and want to celebrate. Can't you just imagine the pride on their faces at the end of the year as they see the gems they mined in their own pieces? And, by the way, you can do the same for yourself, too.

Try On Craft Moves for Size

As a child, I was fascinated by the oddest things, one of which was the cake-sampling process to choose a wedding cake. I daydreamed about small bites of cake in every flavor combination, sampling each one in hopes of finding the perfect bite for the perfect day. I loved (and still do) the idea of a tasting: being surrounded with possibilities, sampling old favorites, exploring new combinations, and simply enjoying each one, taking careful notes along the way. The spirit of a tasting can have dramatic effects on our writing lives, too. I invite you to taste a sampling of mentor texts: to try on all sorts of writing styles and see which ones set your heart on fire and which you didn't even know you loved. Katherine Bomer (2010) created this activity and describes it in her book, *Hidden Gems: Naming and Teaching from the Brilliance in Every Student's Writing.*

Carve out an hour to spend time in your local library or bookstore. Bring your writer's notebook and your cell phone camera. Your task is to wander around, gather a few books that appeal to you, and read them with a writer's eye. If you're not sure where you would begin, borrow some of my favorite mentor texts below:

- *The Relatives Came* by Cynthia Rylant
- *Can I Be Your Dog?* by Troy Cummings
- *How to Make Friends with a Ghost* by Rebecca Green
- *Lily's Purple Plastic Purse* by Kevin Henkes
- *Yo! Yes?* by Chris Raschka
- *Pecan Pie Baby* by Jacqueline Woodson
- *Night of the Veggie Monster* by George McClements
- "Eleven" by Sandra Cisneros
- "Fish Cheeks" by Amy Tan
- "The Jacket" by Gary Soto
- 'Thank You, Ma'am" by Langston Hughes

As you skim through each book, pay careful attention to what the writer does to connect with you and convey meaning across the page. When you notice something, stop and read it again. What about the writer's craft is resonating with you? How does the craft affect you as a reader? Jot down the titles with powerful craft moves in your notebook, and snap a picture of the page showcasing the craft move in action. You can leave these pictures on your device or print them later to add to your page. Put the text you are admiring in your own words. What is the author doing that supports you as a reader and lifts you as a fellow writer? These pages of your notebook will become indispensable tools to fuel your own writing life; you can add to them each time you encounter a text you admire, something you'll be more conscious of in the future as a result.

Next, choose one of the craft moves that resonated most with you, that you are eager to try, or that you have not previously considered. Turn to a clean page in your notebook and have a go of it. Spend a few minutes writing and experimenting. Emulate the craft move you see and try it on for size. How does it feel? What possibilities exist inside your writing life that you might not have known were possible?

Let me give you an example. One of my first pages in my notebook focused on craft moves to emulate from *The Big Orange Splot* by Daniel Pinkwater. In this book, a seagull drops a splot of orange paint on Mr. Plumbean's house, and much to his neighbor's dismay, he decides not only to leave it there but to transform his house into his dreams as a result. Pinkwater repeats these sentences throughout the book that are central to the development of the text: *My house is me and I am it. My house is where I like to be and it looks like all my dreams.* I captured these sentences in my notebook because I loved the sense of hope they provided. I decided to try using repeating text throughout one of my next journal entries. I was having a particularly hard day and was writing to process the events. Each time I wrote of something difficult, I followed up with a single sentence: *But there is always tomorrow.* While it did not emulate the exact structure of Pinkwater's text, it had the same effect. Pinkwater's repetition focused readers on the positive that came from the unlikely orange paint splot on Mr. Plumbean's home: the realization of his dreams. And my repetition focused on the positive that was yet to come: tomorrow was a new day. So, you can literally emulate craft moves and stick closely to what they teach you for your own writing, or you can embody the thinking behind them and apply them to your own words.

If you are up for another challenge, try this: Choose a piece of writing from your writer's notebook, and rewrite the exact same piece, using a new craft move based on your learning. You might rewrite a narrative entry, using more descriptive language, or you might explore formatting and turn it into a poem instead. How does using a new craft move stretch your writing abilities? How does it change how the reader might perceive your message? Which version resonates with you most?

When we read with a writer's eye, we learn from the craft of others and open our writing lives to new possibilities, breathing new life into our work. The same can happen for students.

Here's How to Bring It to the Classroom

Start by sharing the collection you just created, and mine the books for hidden gems together. Then, use those books to support your own writing instruction. Bring them into your writing workshop minilessons or tote them around to your conferences for one-to-one support. Choose your collection strategically based on upcoming units of study or the strengths and needs of your students. Where to begin? I always start my mentor text search at the Moving Writers "Mentor Text Dropbox," an online collection curated by Allison Marchetti and Rebekah O'Dell.

Once students get used to using mentor texts to inspire their own writing, they are more apt to read through the lens of a writer, too. As they find hidden gems in their texts, encourage students to capture them in much the same way you did for yourself:

- Jot the title, author, and craft move on colorful sticky notes to post to a common board in the classroom, or showcase the books on a shelf in the classroom library to discuss during writing instruction.
- Snap a picture of a powerful page or craft move to emulate, and upload it to a shared Padlet wall.
- Record a short Flipgrid video describing the craft move, and snap a picture of the book as the video cover page.

Students can turn to these curated collections when they need inspiration or a helping hand for their own writing pieces. Reading with a writer's eye and noticing brilliant craft moves can greatly boost students' writing stamina, engagement, and motivation, just as it may have done for you.

Participate in Writing Workshops

Each day, you likely invite your students into writing instruction. You likely provide minilessons, invite students to try new craft moves to strengthen their growing writing abilities, and celebrate their work as writers. But when was the last time you sought out opportunities to do the same? Writers, both student and teacher, grow with the support of a more knowledgeable other who can provide lessons, mentor texts, and supportive conferencing. Envision participating in writing workshops for adult writers like yourself, either in person or virtually:

sessions where writers learn through minilessons and workshops hosted by published authors and other writers. Here are a few ways to find one near you:

- Head to your local university and learn about its continuing education programs. You will likely find writing classes and/or writing workshops, both in person and online.
- Connect with your local chapter of the National Writing Project. You'll find writing workshops, seminars, and other opportunities to connect with writers.
- Explore virtual writing workshop opportunities. There are plenty of virtual writing workshops that can help support your writing life. My favorites are those that specifically support teacher–writers, such as TeachWrite, but there are many options depending on what your personal writing goals are. The Writers Studio in New York offers multiple online classes and 24PearlStreet offers online workshops and work groups to connect writers together. The Writer's Digest offers a wide range of classes through their Writer's Digest University, and author Jennifer Serravallo has even offered free reading and writing camp sessions online through the Reading and Writing Strategies Facebook community.
- Join an online learning community, such as Skillshare, where you'll find classes on all aspects of writing, from fifteen-minute mini-sessions to longer classes. You can take part in your own personal writing workshop from the comfort of your home.

You might not be able to participate in a writing workshop today, but you can make plans to try one in the future. The idea is to put ourselves in the shoes of our students, fellow writers who are invited to stretch their writing skills on a daily basis, as soon as we can. Once you try it, you might be surprised at how you feel: anxious to try something new, but excited to learn a new craft; frustrated at your awkward first attempts, then thrilled at your newfound abilities. You'll likely experience the same range of emotions your students do, and you can bring these experiences back to your own teaching to better connect with your students as writers.

Here's How to Bring It to the Classroom

One of the obvious benefits of your participating in a writing workshop is the newfound writing experiences, skills, craft, and confidence you develop, igniting your enthusiasm for writing in a way that cannot be replicated through any other experience. And this changes the entire feel of your writing instruction. You can share your experiences directly with your students, writer to writer: the skills you are learning, the craft techniques you are trying, the pieces you've completed. You might

- bring in aspects of the writing lessons you are experiencing to deepen your own teaching
- use your own writing as mentor texts during minilessons or individual conferences
- share your writing alongside your students during share time so they know what you are working on.

You might even decide to bring new writing mentors into the classroom for your students to experience themselves. Andy Schoenborn, an eleventh- and twelfth-grade teacher, invited local poets to teach minilessons to his students so they could experience new mentors and ways of learning, too. Robert Fanning taught Andy's students a minilesson on his revision process for writing poetry. He walked students through the work of a writer by unveiling the writing, rhetorical choices, and intentional moves he made within a poem. By demonstrating the detailed work involved in poems that seem, on the surface, to be effortless creations, Fanning gave credence to the work Andy asked his students to do while re-envisioning their own work.

Inviting writers into the classroom brings a new level of energy to writing instruction and offers students real-life mentors to follow! And these "visits" do not have to be live events or even live, virtual events. Many authors post writing minilessons for young writers to learn from. Here are a few sites from my collection:

- Authors sharing writing tips on Flipgrid videos: flipgrid.com/authorconnection
- Jess Keating's videos for young writers on YouTube
- Free daily writing videos with author Amy Ludwig VanDerwater: https://padlet.com/AmyLV/oiuzf3l8mdi2

- Mo Willems' LUNCH DOODLE: www.kennedy-center.org/education/mo-willems/lunch-doodles/
- Grace Lin's videos: www.gracelin.com/content.php?page=videos
- "Authors Everywhere!": susantanbooks.com/authors-everywhere-resources

Writing workshops invigorate writing. While nothing can replace our classroom instruction with our own students, bringing a fresh face and new perspective into our instruction can be just the thing our students need to keep their writing motivation high.

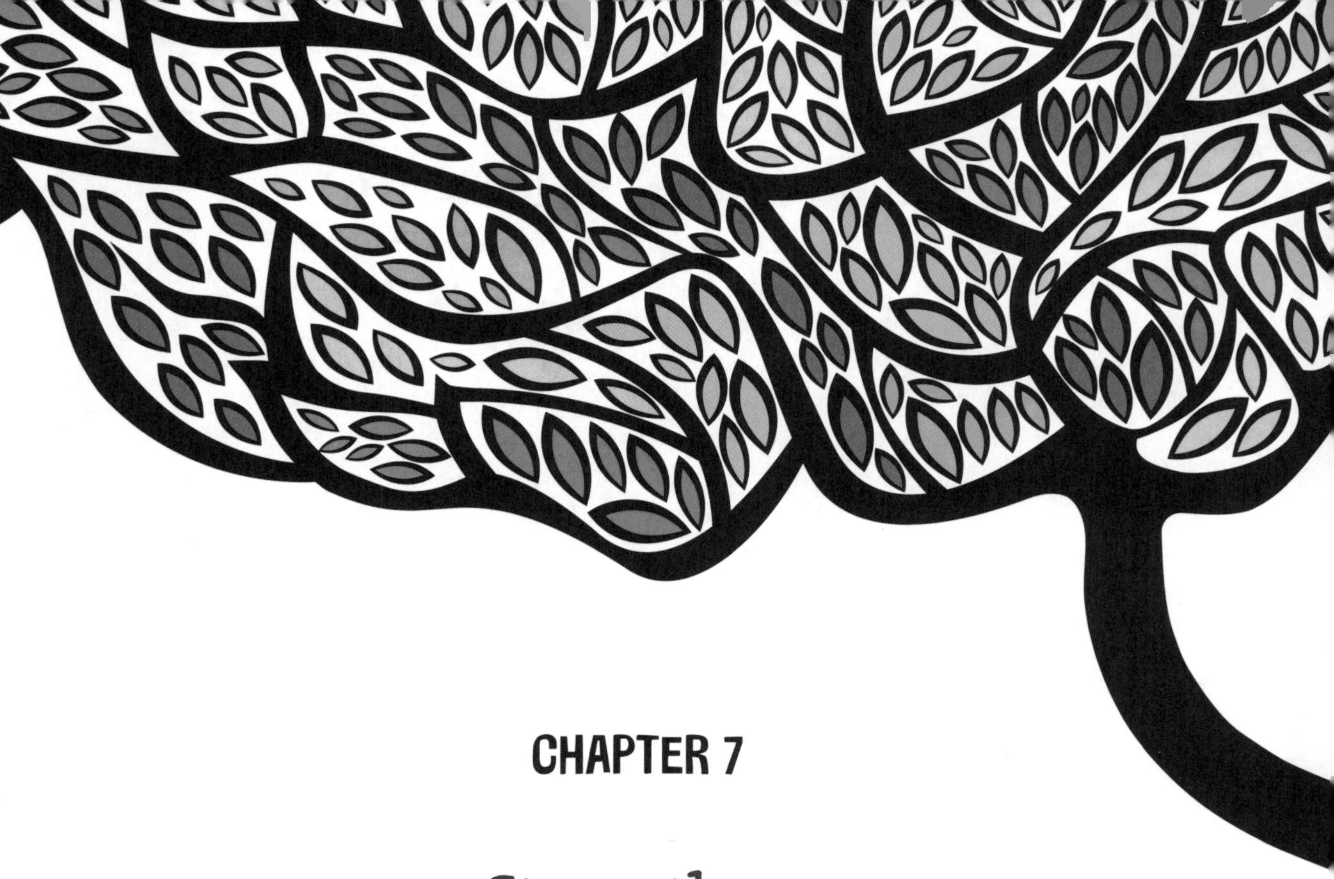

CHAPTER 7

Strengthen Our Writing Communities

It is second nature to immediately reach out to a family member, a friend, or colleagues after we have finished a good book. We can't help but pay the book forward and eagerly look for ways to connect with other readers around it. But that might not be the case with writing. Chances are that when we write something, we keep it close and private. Now, I'm not talking about the text messages, emails, and daily to-do lists. I am talking about the notebook entries, the poems and short stories, the personal reflections in a private diary. Writing is a highly personal process and many choose to keep their writing private. But broadening our writing community to connect with other writers and share pieces of our writerly life grows our writing identities and strengthens our sense of writing community.

Expand Your Personal Writing Network

A community can be loosely defined as a group of people with a common characteristic, interest, or goal. Traditionally, communities were comprised of people who lived close enough to connect and collaborate around common interests. But with the help of technology, social media has broadened the idea of community and made it easier to bring together people who have common goals and interests, including teacher–writers. There are multiple communities of teacher–writers who band together to boost their confidence and writing abilities. These communities can unlock writing potential and possibilities you didn't know you had inside of you. I know because it did the same for me.

Fill Your Writing Feeds

Social media, particularly Twitter or Instagram, is a fountain of writing inspiration. We can personalize our Twitter feeds by creating personalized lists filled with writing inspiration and nuggets of wisdom in three easy steps:

1. Head to your Twitter profile and click on the "lists" icon (it looks like a piece of notebook paper).
2. Create a new list and title it something like "Writing Inspiration" or "Writing Community."
3. Head to the profiles of your favorite writers and writing accounts. Add their feed to your list by clicking on their three dots, and choose the "add to lists" option.

Now, when you head to Twitter, you can simply click on the list you created and instantly browse the feed of the writers you admire. You'll find some of my favorites in Figure 7.1.

While Twitter is my current favorite platform for connecting and collaborating with educators, Instagram is where I get the majority of my writing inspiration. Since each post has an image to correspond to it, my feed is flooded with picture prompts, mentor texts, and bits of writing craft. Start with your favorite authors and illustrators and follow their accounts. They'll often report about their writing days and routines, or share inspiration and even small pieces of their writing or illustrations. You'll find some of the accounts I follow in Figure 7.2.

Author–Writer		Twitter Handle
Ralph Fletcher	→	@FletcherRalph
Anne Lamott	→	@ANNELAMOTT
Writer's Digest	→	@WritersDigest
Jon Winokur	→	@AdviceToWriters
Merriam-Webster	→	@MerriamWebster
Daily Writing Tips	→	@writing_tips
Write to Done	→	@WritetoDone
The Write Life	→	@thewritelife
Book Riot	→	@BookRiot
NaNoWriMo	→	@NaNoWriMo
NY Public Library	→	@nypl

FIGURE 7.1 *Some Twitter accounts I follow for writing inspiration*

Author–Illustrator		Instagram Handle
Rupi Kaur	→	@rupikaur_
Glennon Doyle	→	@glennondoyle
Chimamanda Adichie	→	@chimamanda_adichie
Debbie Ridpath Ohi	→	@inkygirl
Kate Gavino	→	@lastnightsreading
The Write Practice	→	@thewritepractice
K. M. Weiland	→	@authorkmweiland
Cleo Wade	→	@cleowade
Writing Motivation	→	@writingmotivation
Learn with English Shots	→	@englishshots
Grammarly	→	@grammarly

FIGURE 7.2 *Some Instagram accounts of authors and illustrators*

Both Twitter and Instagram use hashtags to curate and organize information. By following a few hashtags dedicated to writing, you'll scroll your way to a more-robust writerly life. There are four kinds of hashtags I like to follow:

- Genre Hashtags: Follow the hashtag feeds of your favorite genre, such as #fantasy or #realisticfiction, etc. You'll find books to read, new authors to explore craft moves with, and fellow writers exploring the genre.
- Process Hashtags: This is where you browse feeds focused on different stages of the writing process (#Revising or #AmEditing, etc.). You'll find solace in the virtual company of other writers in the same phase of the writing process, and you'll likely find resources to support you along the way.
- Creative Hashtags: This is where you'll find writing inspiration. Try #WritingPrompt, #StoryStarter, #WIP (Work in Progress), or #Creativity to launch your writing.
- Hashtags for Writers: These are the hashtags whose sole purpose is to link writers together: #AmWriting, #WritersLife, #TeachWrite, #IndieAuthors, #NaNoWriMo, #WritersBlock, and #LoveWriting.

Here's How to Bring It to the Classroom

One of the best ways to translate inspiration from your writing feeds to the writing community in your classroom is by spotlighting the posts that grabbed your attention. Share the posts, pictures, and links that made you stop scrolling and start writing with your students. Display them on the SMART Board or print them out to add to a physical wall of writing inspiration, mimicking a social media feed. My current favorite is a blog post from Bored Panda that highlights an artist in Bulgaria putting googly eyes on broken street objects (Jurkštaitė 2018). After reading the post, I purchased googly eyes and went for a walk in my neighborhood to create my own. You'll find two of my googly creations in Figure 7.3.

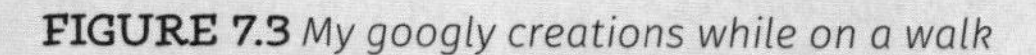

FIGURE 7.3 *My googly creations while on a walk*

You can also bring writing hashtags into your classroom community to spark connection, collaboration, and a little fun. Many teachers keep track of where students are in the writing process with a status-of-the-class routine (Sibberson and Szymusiak 2008). At the start of writing workshop, students call out the stage of the writing process they are currently in. Students could call out their writing process in hashtag form or note their hashtagged process on a sticky note on their desk.

Find Inspiration in Podcasts

As a busy educator and mother, I used to wish that I could just wiggle my nose like Samantha Stephens (any *Bewitched* fans here?) and instantly be transported to my next destination, skipping drives and commutes to save time in my scheduled days. But I've come to enjoy those drive, especially when I am the only one in the car, because I use that time to fill myself up before I arrive at the destination. Sometimes, my commutes are silent. Sometimes, I catch up with others on Bluetooth. But most days, I fill my car rides with podcasts dedicated to reading, writing, and personal growth.

I have a few favorite podcasts dedicated to writing that I eagerly look forward to as I shut the car door, and you can, too. Here are a few of my favorites:

- *Grammar Girl:* This popular podcast hosted by Mignon Fogarty has delightful episodes dedicated to your most-pressing grammar questions.
- *The Writer Files:* Hosted by Kelton Reid, this podcast shares the habits and routines of our beloved authors.
- *A Way with Words:* This podcast explores language examined through the lenses of family, history, and culture.
- *Beautiful Writers Podcast:* Hosted by Linda Sivertsen, this podcast features conversations with some of the most well-recognized writers in the world.
- *Writing Class Radio:* This podcast of a writing class introduces listeners to inspirational stories and ways to write their own.
- *Anne Kroeker: Writing Coach*: This podcast provides listeners with resources and inspiration to become more curious, creative, and productive.
- The Writing University's *Eleventh Hour Podcast*: This podcast features recordings of craft talks by writers of various genres who presented at the Eleventh Hour Lecture Series during the University of Iowa's Summer Writing Festival.

I'm often asked how I keep up with my podcast-listening addiction, and the answer is simple: I don't. Yes, there are a few favorites that I listen to on the day they are released, but I listen to the others as I need them, given my particular goals and activities for the week or month. That's the beauty of the playlist: You can subscribe to as many podcasts as you want—and then listen and learn on your own time and on your own terms. So, choose one from the list above and give an episode a try. Then, take your newfound inspiration to your notebook.

Here's How to Bring It to the Classroom

If you've read the chapters of this book in order, you've already explored using podcasts with students to boost their reading habits. Now we'll explore how podcasts can support students' writing, too. Here are a few podcasts focused on writing and storytelling for children:

- *The Story Seeds*, created by Literary Safari
- *The Music Box*, created by Louisville Public Media
- *Kids Ask Authors*, created by PACYWORKS STUDIO
- *Buttons and Figs*, a podcast for kids about playing with words
- *Story Pirates*, created by Gimlet
- *What If World*, created by Eric O'Keefe

You might start by talking with students about podcasts and how intricately connected they are to the writing process. Podcasts are audio files created on almost any topic imaginable and made available in digital format for automatic download over the Internet. To create one, podcasters have to make a plan for their episode, write a draft or script to record, write supplementary show notes for listeners, and advertise their podcast to share with listeners. Sounds pretty similar to the writing process, right? So, just as we look to authors and mentor texts for writing inspiration in a traditional writing process, we can turn to podcasts for more of the same. Here are a few ideas for bringing podcast writing into your classroom:

https://bit.ly/2IvUPrY

Scan to listen to Kasey Bell's podcast episode on podcasting

- Add a podcast nook in your classroom library or writing station for students to listen to during free time.
- Play clips of particular episodes during morning meetings or related minilessons.
- Play an episode during snack or lunch for those that want to learn while they munch.
- Link episodes to QR codes on your weekly newsletters for families.

If you find that your students are getting hooked, consider creating a class podcast of your own! Students can work through the entire writing process, learn new digital tools in the process, and have a real, authentic audience for their work. Kasey Bell of Shake Up Learning created a podcast episode to support teachers ready to create their own podcast with students. Access it by scanning the QR code.

Soundtrap EDU has also compiled a set of helpful resources for teachers looking to explore podcasting with their students, which you can access through the QR code.

Whether you use podcasts for writing inspiration or are inspired to create a podcast with your class, your students are sure to enjoy this digital format that might better resemble their digital media consumption outside of school.

https://bit.ly/35nWw3o

Scan for a collection of podcasting resources from Soundtrap

Join an Online Writing Community

While I always love a good face-to-face conversation, my virtual writing communities are what boost my identity as a writer, strengthen my writing habit, and offer plenty of inspiration along the way. My engagement in these communities goes beyond passively following writers and hashtags on social media to actively connecting, sharing, and collaborating with others around our writing lives. Here are some of my favorite teacher–writer communities that are worth checking out:

- The National Writing Project (NWP): The NWP is a leading organization for educators dedicated to advancing writing instruction. Supporting both teachers and students as writers, the NWP offers local project sites, online blog posts, articles, and additional opportunities to learn and grow through its social media communities on Facebook, Twitter, and Instagram.
- The Writing Cooperative: Their mission is simple—to help fellow members write better. They offer free and paid subscription articles, a Slack community for contributors, and writing challenges to keep you on your writing toes (more about that next). They offer inspiration, helpful tips, and mentor texts to spark thinking and writing.
- TeachWrite: This organization specializes in helping teachers and their students grow as writers and believes that teachers who write learn about writing from the inside out, making them

more effective teachers of writing. TeachWrite offers multiple opportunities to find the level of support you need, and its free Facebook group is a good place to start. Each day, Jennifer Laffin posts a word of the day to prompt you to write and encourages you to celebrate your writing with the group.

- Teachers Write: Kate Messner offers a free summer writing camp for teachers and librarians. Teacher–writers learn from mentor texts, talk about writing craft, and chat with the authors of those mentor texts to boost their writing lives over the summer.
- 100 Days of Summer Writing: Allison Marchetti and Rebekah O'Dell offer teachers 100 days of mentor-text-based summer writing inspiration to spark writing. Each day brings a new image or text prompt to explore in your writer's notebook, and some teachers even bring their students into the project! This is a great way to fuel your writing in the slower days of summer.

You might find inspiration simply from following online, but the real gains will come when you take a risk and join in. Take a few moments to explore the communities I shared, or do a quick Google search to find others. There is no one right way to participate in these communities, and there is no one judging the quantity and quality of your participation. Just take one step: follow a new social media account, join a Facebook group, or simply bookmark the site on your browser for later exploration. Every step counts and leads somewhere.

Here's How to Bring It to the Classroom

Once you've spent some time boosting your own writing communities, think about the writing communities you have created in your classroom. Can students choose to work with a partner or a small group? Can they seek out classmates for support on particular writing strategies or craft moves? Do they know where to go when they are stuck and need inspiration? One way to support these kinds of connections is to create a "Find Me!" board to celebrate the risks students are taking in their writing. How does it work? Students take a sticky note, and label it with their name and one thing they have been working on as a writer that they could help other writers with, such as coming up with writing topics, developing characters, using quotation marks, editing, etc. They post these sticky notes on the bulletin board for others to review. When students have a writing challenge, rather than try to go it alone, they can glance at the board to see if one of their classmates has already solved that challenge and can help. As students' writing prowess grows, they can update their sticky notes for renewed partnerships.

The important thing is to take the lessons you have learned about your own writing life and use them to make authentic changes in your classroom. When we remove ourselves from the process of writing and simply become teachers of writing, we forget how powerful, invigorating, frustrating, scary, and exhilarating writing can be. But when we live as writers, we understand firsthand what our students are experiencing. Working with students as fellow writers, and not as teachers with the right answer, we form powerful learning communities that grow in writing together.

Connect with Other Writers

We all have our own comfortable writing preferences: when and where we write, how and what we write, and who we share our writing with. If we are not careful, however, we can fall into writing habits that keep our writing lives exactly where they currently are without forward movement. And if we stay in our own lane, so to speak, we miss out on the potential of what we have yet to discover in our writing lives. If I had never attended a state literacy conference, I would have never learned the descriptive writing techniques from Charles R. Smith Jr., author of *I Am America*, that sparked my memoir writing. If I hadn't attended a virtual writing workshop session, I might have never realized how much I loved storytelling. And if I hadn't taken a chance with new authors, I would have never found the power of their words to impact my own. Writing involves taking risks in our own learning, ones that push us past our current boundaries and invite us into new ways of thinking, being, and showing up to the page.

Pair with a Writing Partner

Writing may be a solo act, but it's a social experience. Having someone to check in with regularly, bounce ideas off of, and even share writing pieces with is an important step in growing your personal writing community. Let's take a closer look at how you can pair with a writing partner, both in person and virtually:

- Think about the people and educators you interact with on a daily basis that might be interested in partnering together: your partner, friends, family, neighbors, colleagues, etc. Ideally, you'll find someone who is also looking to grow their writing life, but it is perfectly acceptable to partner with someone who is not a writer. In exchange, you could help them stay accountable to their own personal goals.
- Partner with local writing organizations to give you a dose of accountability. I recommend looking up your local chapter of the National Writing Project to see how you can become involved. Your local library or bookstore may also have a writing group that you could learn more about. Professional organizations, such as the International Literacy Association, the National Council for Teachers of English, and the Collaborative Blogging Project, also offer opportunities to connect with other educators who share the same interests and passions.
- Head online. Use social media to find a potential writing partner. Ask for ideas, tips, and resources—and share your own. You might be surprised by the relationships that result. In fact, a single tweet connected me with Kris McGee, my writing partner; without it, our connection might have never been made. Browse hashtags dedicated to teacher–writers and writing teachers. Here are a few of my favorites: #TeachWrite, #TeachersWrite, #TCRWPchat. As you browse the feeds, you'll find inspiring tweets and posts from other teacher–writers. Follow them. Like their posts. Tell them how much their contributions mean to your own writing life. Validate their courage to share their writing with the world, and band together with them to do the same.

Here's How to Bring It to the Classroom

Once you see the power of a writing partnership, you'll likely want to bring the same to your students. Far too often, I see writing partnerships in classrooms that are focused on editing. Partners swap writing pieces to read for clarity and edit their classmates' pieces with an editing checklist. But this is not the main purpose of a writing partnership. Writing partnerships give us writing ideas, provide inspiration and cheerleading, help us navigate through challenges, and celebrate our writing identities. Here are a few ways to do just that, which take little preparation but yield powerful results:

- Create writing partners. Pair students together to offer support and ideas for writing. While each student in a pair writes independently, partners can motivate each other, ask for writing advice, and provide an ear to listen to a piece.
- Create writing buddies. Pair your students with a cross-grade writing partner. Students in the younger grade get to team with more-experienced writers, and the older students have the chance to showcase their writing and teach the younger students what they know about writing.
- Harness the power of technology to connect with other classrooms around the world. Use social media to find an interested teacher, and introduce your classes to each other virtually. You might work on shared projects, come together for a virtual sharing session. or simply connect around your work together as writers.

Start a Writing Group

Writing groups are small groups of dedicated writers who cheer each other on, hold members accountable to their writing goals, share drafts of their current writing with each other, and broaden their current writing boundaries with the support of the group. I have been part of multiple writing groups over time: my lesson-planning group as an undergraduate, my doctoral writing (and support) group, the writing groups I host as part of my graduate teaching, and the small writing groups I choose to be part of currently. These groups may be short-term groups designed to jump-start your writing life or help you tackle unfinished writing projects. Or, you might be lucky enough to become part of a writing group that sticks together over time. Depending on the participants, the groups might meet frequently or less often, involve food and spirits, and even include strategy sessions to push the writing forward. So, how can you get a group started?

1. Invite fellow teacher–writers to get together to talk about writing. If you have a writing partner, start there and invite other interested educators.
2. Set a date for an initial meeting, either local or virtual, and kick off your first session with light conversation. An in-person meeting could take place after school in a classroom, at a local coffee shop on a Saturday morning, or at a favorite bookstore for inspiration.
3. Decide on a format and structure for the group and create a loose agenda. You might start with introductions, share your writing dreams, and imagine a vision for the group based on your own hopes and preferences. Will you meet weekly? Monthly? Will you write together or talk about your writing? Will you read drafts of each other's work or talk about challenges and solutions? Are there certain ground rules or norms you want to set?
4. After your writing group has met a few times and is running smoothly, try something new to keep things fresh and creative. You might try a creative writing exercise, share mentor texts for inspiration, attend an author event or writing workshop together, or simply gather for some social fun.
5. Consider adding digital tools to support members in between meetings. You might have weekly email check-ins or connect on social media. I highly recommend Voxer, a mobile messaging app that combines text, voice, photo, and video messages for powerful collaboration.
6. Celebrate! Take time to celebrate your commitment, your developing writing relationships with others, and your strengthened identity as a writer.

Here's How to Bring It to the Classroom

Classroom writing groups can provide a heightened sense of community for students as well. Their fellow writers can help generate writing ideas, work through challenges, and cheer one another on from the sidelines. Consider forming groups such as the following:

- Strategy Groups: For these groups, you bring together students who are working on the same strategy as their goal or who need additional support on a strategy.
- Process Groups: You can group students together who are working on the same stage of the writing process to help move them along and to model strategies.
- Content Groups: These groups bring students together who are working on similar topics to help generate content and ideas.
- Genre Groups: You can bring students together who are writing within the same genre to teach genre-specific skills.
- Support Groups: Students can form voluntary partnerships or small groups to simply support each other as writers.

It's also important to give students the experience of sharing their writerly life with others not in their classroom, just as you did. Consider finding a class to connect with virtually around writing and writing instruction. You could collaborate with another teacher around units of study, lesson planning, and more.

Enjoy a Writing Retreat

Writing retreats are just as they sound: indulgent opportunities to retreat away from the hustle and bustle of daily life and focus on reading, writing, and relaxing. Some retreats offer daylong, weekend-long, or weeklong spaces to unplug, unwind, and cultivate your writing life. Writers spend long stretches of time writing, exploring writing craft, and working on personal writing goals.

Spend some time exploring a few nationally known retreats that are currently on my personal bucket list:

- Retreat & Create: Alexis Grant, founder of the popular website *The Write Life,* leads a retreat in the historic mountain town of Harpers Ferry, West Virginia. This small, women-only retreat invites all career-focused women who need space and quiet to focus on their work, including writing.
- Autumn Writing Retreat in the Berkshires: Page Lambert, an instructor of creative writing at the University of Denver's graduate school, leads writing sessions and individual consultations throughout the weeklong stay.
- The White Mountain Book Writing Retreat blends yoga, healthy eating, and writing together for an overall nourishing experience. Held in the mountains of New Hampshire, Dorothy Holtermann leads nonfiction writers through group classes and private coaching.
- Jess Lourey's writing retreats: These women-only writing retreats usually include group workshops and private coaching sessions along with meditation, yoga, and relaxation.

The allure of a writing retreat revolves around uninterrupted time to write, the removal of everyday distractions, and a calm atmosphere to help you recharge your mind and dive into your writing. The retreats I mentioned can certainly provide all of that, but you can easily bring the spirit of a writing retreat to your home. Block off an hour or two over the weekend to retreat from the demands of your life and write. Find a babysitter for the kids, turn off all media, put your phone on silent mode, bring a pitcher of lemonade and your writing materials to your backyard, and write in the hammock. Or, curl up in your favorite chair, turn the television off, turn on soft music, and give yourself the gift of a solid hour to write. My favorite DIY writing retreat involves getting up early in the morning when the house is still asleep. I pour myself a cup of coffee, grab my laptop, and write for a solid hour or two, watching the sunrise, if I'm lucky. These small, individual retreats may not be glamorous, but they are productive.

If you'd like, you can invite others into your DIY retreat. Invite fellow teacher–writers together for an afternoon of writing. This might be at your home, at a local coffee shop, or in a meeting room at your local library. Bring snacks and drinks, your writing materials, and a commitment to unplug from your devices (unless you write best by typing). Begin with conversation and share your writing goals for the session. Then, simply write. Write for long stretches of time and take movement breaks when needed. End by coming together for a share session: share your thoughts, writing, and process. Learn from each other and gain inspiration. And then set a date to schedule another mini-retreat.

You might even create a pop-up writing retreat. Head online, tag a few fellow educators on your favorite social media platform, and see who is up for an impromptu writing retreat. Connect online through Zoom or Google Hangouts and share your writing goals. Spend some time writing with your laptop open, checking in with the group periodically so you're not distracted by the laundry or by any number of other tasks competing for your attention. End after a set period of time by sharing your writing, and make plans for future retreats. A writing retreat, small or large, can be just the thing you need to renew your commitment to writing and strengthen your writing community.

Here's How to Bring It to the Classroom

Create a retreat-like experience for students without ever leaving school grounds. Surprise students with a trip outside to write with nature. Invite students to bring their notebooks, Chromebooks, and/or clipboards outside and find a place that looks inspiring to them. Have students observe, write, and talk among nature, coming together to share at the end.

Shelley Fenton and Krista Senatore of Lit Coach Connection decided to host writing cafés and retreats for their middle-school students. They transformed classrooms into cafés complete with tablecloths and soft music, and offered students thirteen different writing stations to choose from. Students created heart maps (Heard 2016), played with objects to spark stories, explored burning questions, wrote song lyrics, created inspirational memes, and more. Students chose the stations that interested them most and left the café with at least three new entries in their writer's notebook. They even raffled off prizes to continue their writing life: new notebook, writing utensils, sticky notes, and more. To view the videos showcasing the entire process, open your Internet web search and type in "Lit Coach Connection." Once you're on the home page, search for "writing cafes." The project has since expanded, and students are invited to explore their writing hearts through poetry cafés as well.

Broaden Your Writing Boundaries

I am a great fan of Anne Lamott, and her book *Bird by Bird* had a tremendous impact on my beliefs about writing and writers. When writing about the role that publication plays in a writer's life, she used a quote from *Cool Runnings,* the movie about the first Jamaican bobsled team. The team was desperate for an Olympic medal, but their coach reminded them: "If you're not enough before the gold medal, you won't be enough with it" (Lamott 1994, 203). The primary goal of building a writerly life is not formal publication. While getting published is certainly something to aspire to, it is the process of writing that changes who we are, regardless of who sees our words.

Still, we might desire an audience. For some writers, simply sharing personal reflections with trusted friends and family members is enough to fuel their writing. For others, sharing education-related thoughts and ideas through social media is helpful for staying motivated and engaged. Some create a blog to share and connect with others. Others might hope to pursue more traditional publishing, such as writing an article for a magazine or journal or even publishing a book. We each have a voice that has something to share with the world, whether it be our lesson ideas, family recipes, or knack for creating Top 10 lists. And when we do so, we publicly claim our status as a writer and broaden our writing boundaries, one page at a time.

Try a Writing Experiment

As writers, we have all sorts of preferences that make each of us unique: from where and when we write to how and what we write. And while those preferences can launch us into successful writing experiences, they can also hold us back from trying something new as writers. Enter writing experiments.

First, let's uncover our writing preferences. Turn to a fresh page in your writer's notebook, and title it: "I am the kind of writer who. . ." Spend some time thinking about your preferences as a writer and then jot down the ideas that come to mind. Here are a few prompts to get you started:

- Where and when do you like to write most?
- What do you like to write about?
- What kinds of writing are you most proud of?
- How do you write? What is your writing process?
- What brings joy to your writing life?

After spending some time reflecting, choose an experiment to explore your writing life in more depth. Move outside your writing boundaries, and experiment with different writing times, locations, styles, formats, and content. Choose a new writing practice and see what you find out about yourself. And don't knock it until you try it—you never know how your writing life might respond! Figure 7.4 offers a few ways to experiment.

Where We Write	
at a table or desk	at a local coffee shop
curled up in a chair or sofa	at your local library
outside with the breeze	at a public park
When We Write	
early morning before the day begins	in bursts of waiting (for appointments, for children, etc.)
right before bed	scheduled into your day
on a lunch break	impromptu writing whenever the opportunity arises
How We Write	
on blank pages	with soft background noise
on lined paper	with a drink or snack
on a computer or device	alone
with text-to-speech software	with a writing partner or in a writing group
with silence	
What We Write	
fiction	realistic fiction
nonfiction	historical fiction
lists	for ourselves
observations	for an audience

FIGURE 7.4 *Ways to experiment with your writing life*

Be open to discovering new ideas about your writing life. I always thought morning writing worked best for me, but I found I'm most productive during shorter bursts of unexpected writing time. I used to think that I needed silence to write, but when I tried writing with soft music playing in the background, it energized me and I felt more creative.

After trying a few experiments for a while, turn to the next clean page in your notebook and title it: "Now, I am the kind of writer who . . ." Based on what you learned about yourself, add to your list. What did you find out about yourself as a writer that you didn't know before? How did your small experiments strengthen your identity as a writer?

Here's How to Bring It to the Classroom

Far too often, in schools, writing is something that students must complete rather than a process they live. Writing in school is often dictated by the curriculum or the teacher: when and how often students write, where and how they plan and draft, and what they are able to write about. Based on what you just uncovered about your writing preferences, would you thrive as a writer in your current classroom? How does your classroom support the kind of writer who

- prefers to draw and sketch seed ideas for writing pieces instead of completing a graphic organizer
- writes more productively when typing (instead of handwriting) ideas and drafts
- revises throughout the drafting process, not only at the end of a draft
- needs to physically manipulate the text, adding sticky notes, cutting apart sentences and rearranging them, rather than compose entirely on a computer
- feels uncomfortable sharing writing with others
- finds it difficult to get ideas onto the page and needs more thinking time before writing freely?

Our classrooms must support all kinds of students who have different abilities, preferences, and habits as writers. If students do not feel that their own personal ways of writing are valued, then chances are they will choose *not to* write or, at the very least, become detached from the process. So, how can you make small changes to your classroom that honor a flexible writing process? Dedicate class time to experiment with students' writing preferences, and find areas where you could add a bit of flexibility to your writing routines. Here are a few possibilities:

- Create different writing zones in your classroom. Honor students who need flat surfaces, comfortable writing spots, soft background music, or complete silence (as much as you can in a classroom) as they write.
- Honor preferences in writing materials. Give students control over what they write with: keyboards versus writing utensils, lined paper versus blank paper, pens versus pencils.
- Provide multiple writing scaffolds. Graphic organizers work well for some students but not for others. And certain graphic organizers might motivate some students but hinder others. Model, teach, and provide students with multiple writing tools, and allow them to choose the one that works best for them based on their own preferences and the type of piece they are working on.
- Rethink requirements. Allow students to choose the writing tools that work best for them. Provide options for publication, such as handwritten or typed pieces, presentations or more creative products.

We all have writing preferences that honor our growing identities and fuel our motivation and confidence. If those writing preferences are *not* acknowledged, valued, and supported, chances are that writing will not be something kept close to our hearts and threaded through our lives.

Participate in a Writing Challenge

The word *challenge* may conjure up competitive images or something hard that you need to work through; that is not the kind of writing challenge I am talking about here. Writing challenges are opportunities to own your identity as a writer, to join a community of fellow writers working to boost their habits or writing craft, and to challenge your writing life in a way that fits your strengths and goals as a writer. They are personal challenges fueled by a community cheering you on.

Here are just a few challenges you might explore to do the same for yourself:

- The Slice of Life Challenge is spearheaded by *Two Writing Teachers,* a collaborative blog that offers teachers a wide variety of resources, ideas, and communities to support their writing habit. The challenge began in 2008 and offers teachers three ways to contribute: by sharing their stories every Tuesday, by committing to daily writing in the month of March, and by inviting students into a blogging challenge.
- The StoryADay challenge is a monthlong short-story challenge where writers write (and finish!) a short story every day in May. Led by Julie Duffy, writers celebrate their efforts by posting to the community group, often sharing the actual story they produced. This challenge builds a writing habit over time and connects writers with others who hold the same aspirations and are exploring storytelling craft.
- The 52-Week Writing Challenge is a longer-term, but highly personal, challenge. The Writing Cooperative urges writers to commit to writing one thing each week. You choose the thing: a poem, short story, letter, movie review, book recommendation, etc. You can publish your writing on your own blog site or simply share your weekly accomplishment on social media. I love this challenge because it is incredibly personal and based on weekly, rather than daily, writing goals, which I am better suited to accomplish.
- National Novel Writing Month (NaNoWriMo): This writing challenge takes place each November and challenges writers to write a 50,000-word novel in thirty days. While this may seem daunting, it is doable when you break down the challenge into about 1,667 words per day. The NaNoWriMo community is incredibly supportive. It helps you track and share your progress, offers inspirational interviews with well-known writers, and

provides other motivational tools. And if poetry is more your style, National Poetry Writing Month (NaPoWriMo) takes place every April and challenges writers to create thirty poems in thirty days.

- 12 × 12: If you've been dreaming of writing a picture book, then this challenge is for you. Julie Hedlund challenges writers to write twelve picture books in twelve months. Unlike the other challenges, writers pay for community support: writer's forums, online discussions, and even access to agents. I haven't purchased access to this community, but I've challenged myself to draft those stories on my own instead and follow the 12 × 12 social media accounts for accountability and inspiration.
- #100DaysofNotebooking: In this Facebook community page, officially launched on January 1, 2020, Michelle Hasteltine joyfully challenges writers to show up to the page each and every day. Writers share their notebook pages with the #100DaysofNotebooking Facebook community across other social media platforms as well. Speaking from experience, this group can truly change the way you feel about writing and instantly invites you into a community of supportive teacher–writers.

Now, you might hesitate to join a writing challenge because you doubt your ability to successfully follow through for the duration of the challenge. But the act of showing up to the challenge in the first place means you've made the conscious decision to broaden your community of writers. What happens next is icing on the cake.

Some of these challenges can be recreated right within your school and district, too! Jill Davidson, a literacy coordinator in New Brunswick, Canada, created a writing challenge to build a community of teacher–writers across her geographically diverse district. How did she do it? She created a monthly calendar of writing ideas and topics and sent a daily email to the teachers with a reminder to write. You'll find one of the daily challenges in Figure 7.5.

For this challenge, the teachers were invited to share their writing using the #ASDWWrites hashtag, and they reflected on new insights into themselves as writers and teachers of writing. Some even made plans to bring the same no-strings-attached writing opportunities to their students.

Day 17 of a 30-Day Writing Habit

"You should write because you love the shape of stories and sentences and the creation of different words on a page. Writing comes from reading, and reading is the finest teacher of how to write."
Annie Proulx

Today's invitation to write is this open letter. You might choose to:

- write your own open letter,
- reflect on something the letter inspires in you,
- choose a word, image, or phrase to write from,
- use the structure or organization as a model for your own writing,
- try out a craft move or writing technique you notice,
- let your writing go wherever your thinking takes you.

Here is our post on using open letters as mentor texts from the Try this Tomorrow category of MarginNotes.ca.

Happy Writing!

FIGURE 7.5 *An example of Jill Davidson's daily writing challenge for teachers*

Here's How to Bring It to the Classroom

Bring the spirit of a writing challenge to your classroom:

- Re-create any of the challenges I mentioned with your own students, making modifications to fit your students' grade and interests. You can participate in real time or schedule your version of the challenge when it works best for your classroom.
- Create your own classroom challenge based on the writing interests, strengths, and goals of your current students. Here are a few possibilities: A Week Without Tired Words, Small Moment Monday, Ten Days of Lists, A Page a Day, Five Days of Fiction.

- Create personal writing challenges for students. Just as you did when setting personal writing goals, base these challenges on students' unique writing journeys, but with an added incentive of a community. Each day, students tackle their own personal challenge and share their progress with classmates.

Regardless of the challenge you choose, the sole reason to participate in a writing challenge isn't to complete it (although we certainly hope and plan to). It is to come together with a community of other writers working on the same goal. Writing challenges spark camaraderie, support, and inspiration among fellow writers, regardless of the outcome.

Go Public by Blogging

One of my favorite times of the day is early in the morning sipping my first cup of coffee while scrolling through my Bloglovin' email, an email filled with the latest posts of my favorite bloggers. There are some important benefits to blogging, both personal and professional. You can

- improve your writing by telling your personal stories
- connect with other thought leaders in the field (Yes, you are one. If you have thoughts and share them widely, you are leading the way.)
- hold yourself accountable to a writing life
- reflect on your own teaching, learning, and growth
- boost your motivation for writing and teaching
- inspire other educators by documenting your teaching life
- build your personal learning network and writing community.

Blogging gives you a personalized, public outlet to share your writing with the world. You control the site, content, and privacy settings, allowing you to share your voice as you see fit. Here are a few simple steps to launch your own blog:

1. Identify your niche. What do you want to blog about? Education-related topics? A personal hobby? Or, do you want to create a general space to share your writing? Imagine the content of your blog and choose a name. Google it to make sure it isn't already taken.

2. Choose a platform. Blogger and WordPress are two popular platforms to begin with. Choose a theme and design, and consider adding tools and widgets to customize your site.
3. Create your first post. You can post what you are currently writing, share examples of your teaching practice, or even post pictures of your writing notebook.
4. Decide whether to share. If you prefer, you can keep your blog completely private and write for yourself. Or, you can choose to restrict access to specific readers or those you share the link with. Then, when you are ready, you can make your blog public and share it on your social media channels.

You can set up a blog in under thirty minutes using stock templates and simple theme designs. Once you get more comfortable with the platform, you can design and customize your site. Organizations such as the National Blogging Collaborative can support your efforts, too.

Here's How to Bring It to the Classroom

Your students can also experience the same benefits of blogging. By blogging together in the classroom, they can develop writerly habits, boost their writing abilities, explore their more creative side, and increase their communication skills as they interact with authentic audiences. You might blog together as a class and post monthly contributions from each student over time. Or, you might set up individual blogs for your students to share their work individually. Sites such as Edublogs and Kidblog offer student blogging platforms with heightened privacy controls and the option for you to approve and decline posts.

Imagine for a moment how your writing life, and possibly even your life in general, would be different if you experienced the power of sharing your writing with an audience early on in your academic career. In my writing class, I challenge my graduate students to think about the teachers that influenced their writing life over the years. Each one of my students can remember with detail, even years and years later, the experiences that both helped and hindered their writing success. I imagine you can, too. Why not be the teacher that helps your students see their writing potential and works to share it with the world—and even change it?

REFERENCES

Alberto, Sarah. 2018. *The Art of Doodle Words: Turn Your Everyday Doodles into Cute Hand Lettering!* Minneapolis: The Quarto Group.

Ayres, Ruth. 2019. "Heart-Zapper." *Ruth Ayres Writes* (blog), October 2. https://ruthayreswrites.com/2019/10/02/heart-zapper.

Ball, Lanny. 2018. "4 Purposes for a Writer's Notebook: Notebooks as a Writer's Tool." *Two Writing Teachers* (blog), November 7. https://twowritingteachers.org/2018/11/07/4-purposes-for-writers-notebook.

Bogel, Anne. 2018. *I'd Rather Be Reading: The Delights and Dilemmas of the Reading Life*. Ada, MI: Baker Books.

Bomer, Katherine. 2010. *Hidden Gems: Naming and Teaching from the Brilliance in Every Student's Writing*. Portsmouth, NH: Heinemann.

Brookfield, Stephen D. 1995. *Becoming a Critically Reflective Teacher*. San Francisco: Jossey-Bass.

Burkins, Jan, and Kim Yaris. 2018. "Being 'Inspired' to Hold on to New Learning." *CCIRA Professional Development Blog*, September 18. https://ccira.blog/2018/09/18/being-inspired-to-hold-on-to-new-learning.

Chu, Charles. 2017. "In the Time You Spend on Social Media Each Year, You Could Read 200 Books." *Quartz*, January 20. https://qz.com/895101/in-the-time-you-spend-on-social-media-each-year-you-could-read-200-books.

Clear, James. 2018. *Atomic Habits: An Easy & Proven Way to Build Good Habits & Break Bad Ones*. New York: Avery.

Cole, Ardra L., and J. Gary Knowles. 2000. *Researching Teaching: Exploring Teacher Development Through Reflexive Inquiry*. Boston: Allyn and Bacon.

Connor, Janet. 2009. *Writing Down Your Soul: How to Activate and Listen to the Extraordinary Voice Within*. Newburyport, MA: Conari Press.

Curry, Ariel. 2019. "How to Track Your Reading Data." *One Little Library* (blog), January 22.

Dewey, John. 1933. *How We Think: A Restatement of the Relation of Thinking to the Education Process*. Boston: D.C. Heath.

Dozier, Cheryl. 2006. *Responsive Literacy Coaching*. Portsmouth, NH: Stenhouse.

Duhigg, Charles. 2012. *The Power of Habit: Why We Do What We Do in Life and Business*. New York: Random House.

Duckworth, Sylvia. 2018. "Five Ways to Develop a Doodling Culture in Class." *Sylvia Duckworth* (blog), November 20. https://sylviaduckworth.com/2018/11/20/5-ways-to-create-a-doodling-culture-in-your-classroom.

———. 2020. "Sketchnoting for Beginners." https://docs.google.com/presentation/d/1a0TgYBEEQlMv6umZJ_g3KLHGOi1Vv40PHsFhjCN3LkE/edit#slide=id.g3b61d45d09_0_211.

Ebarvia, Tricia. 2017. "How Inclusive Is Your Literacy Classroom Really?" *Heinemann* (blog). https://blog.heinemann.com/heinemann-fellow-tricia-ebavaria-inclusive-literacy-classroom-really.

Fletcher, Ralph. 1996. *A Writer's Notebook*. New York: Harper Trophy.

———. 2017. *Joy Write: Cultivating High-Impact, Low-Stakes Writing*. Portsmouth, NH: Heinemann.

Golub, Marcia. 1999. *I'd Rather Be Writing: A Guide to Finding More Time, Getting More Organized, Completing More Projects and Having More Fun*. Des Moines, IA: Writer's Digest Books.

Heard, Georgia. 2016. *Heart Maps*. Portsmouth, NH: Heinemann.

Jewett, Pamela C. 2011. "'Some People Do Things Different from Us': Exploring Personal and Global Cultures in a First Grade Class." *Journal of Children's Literature* 37 (1): 20–29.

Johnson, Pat, and Katie Keier. 2010. *Catching Readers Before They Fall*. Portsmouth, NH: Stenhouse.

Jurkštaitė, Dominyka. 2018. "Someone in Bulgaria Is Putting Googly Eyes on Broken Street Objects, and It's Even Better Than Fixing Things." *Bored Panda* (community post).

Kaback, Suzy. 2016. "The Draw-a-Reader Test: Informal Assessment Supporting Teacher Inquiry." *Choice Literacy.* www.choiceliteracy.com/articles-detail-view.php?id=391.

Krementz, Jill. 1996. *The Writer's Desk.* New York: Random House Publishing Group.

Lamott, Anne. 1994. *Bird by Bird: Some Instructions on Writing and Life.* New York: Anchor.

Lifshitz, Jessica. 2016. "Having Students Analyze Our Classroom Library to See How Diverse It Is." *Crawling Out of the Classroom* (blog), May 7. https://crawlingoutoftheclassroom.wordpress.com/2016/05/07/having-students-analyze-our-classroom-library-to-see-how-diverse-it-is.

McGregor, Tanny. 2019. *Ink and Ideas.* Portsmouth, NH: Heinemann.

Merriam-Webster Dictionary. 2020a. "Circle" www.merriam-webster.com/dictionary/circle.

———. 2020b. "Commonplace" www.merriam-webster.com/dictionary/commonplace?utm_campaign=sd&utm_medium=serp&utm_source=jsonld.

———. 2020c. "Curiosity" www.merriam-webster.com/dictionary/curiosity

———. 2020d. "Reflection" www.merriam-webster.com/dictionary/reflection?utm_campaign=sd&utm_medium=serp&utm_source=jsonld.

Minor, Cornelius. 2018. *We Got This. Equity, Access, and the Quest to Be Who Our Students Need Us to Be.* Portsmouth, NH: Heinemann.

Mraz, Kristine, Alison Porcelli, and Cheryl Tyler. 2016. *Purposeful Play: A Teacher's Guide to Igniting Deep and Joyful Learning Across the Day.* Portsmouth, NH: Heinemann.

Mulligan, Tammy, and Clare Landrigan. 2018. *It's All About the Books: How to Create Bookrooms and Classroom Libraries That Inspire Readers.* Portsmouth, NH: Heinemann.

National Council for Teachers of English. 2020. "Why I Write Toolkit." https://whyiwrite.us/toolkit.

Parks, Bitsy. 2017. "Increasing Read-Alouds in the Primary Grades." *Choice Literacy.* https://choiceliteracy.com/article/increasing-read-alouds-in-the-primary-grades.

Rief, Linda. 2014. *Read Write Teach: Choice and Challenge in the Reading-Writing Workshop.* Portsmouth, NH: Heinemann.

Roberts, Kate, and Maggie Beattie Roberts. 2016. *DIY Literacy: Teaching Tools for Differentiation, Rigor, and Independence.* Portsmouth, NH: Heinemann.

Rosenthal, Amy Krouse. (@missamykr). 2013. "for anyone trying to discern what to do w/ their life: PAY ATTENTION TO WHAT YOU PAY ATTENTION TO. that's pretty much all the info u need." Twitter, March 15, 2013, 10:02 am. https://twitter.com/missamykr/status/312564535242395648?lang=en.

Sackton, Laura. 2017. "50 DIY Reading Challenges to Make 2018 the Best Year of Your Reading Life." *Book Riot,* December 11. https://bookriot.com/diy-reading-challenges.

Scholastic. 2018. "11 Essentials for a Highly Effective Classroom Library." *Teaching Tools,* August 14. www.scholastic.com/teachers/teaching-tools/articles/11-essentials-for-a-highly-effective-classroom-library.html.

———. 2019. "Reading Partnerships." Unit Plan by Beth Newingham. https://www.scholastic.com/teachers/unit-plans/teaching-content/reading-partnerships/.

Schön, Donald A. 1987. *Educating the Reflective Practitioner: Toward a New Design for Teaching and Learning in the Professions.* Jossey-Bass Higher Education Series. San Francisco: Jossey-Bass.

Serravallo, Jennifer. 2015. *The Reading Strategies Book.* Portsmouth, NH: Heinemann.

Sharp, Colby, ed. 2018. *The Creativity Project: An Awesometastic Story Collection.* New York: Little, Brown.

Short, Kathy G. 2008. "WOW Stories: Connections from the Classroom." *Worlds of Words.* https://wowlit.org/on-line-publications/stories/storiesi2/5/.

Sibberson, Franki, and Karen Szymusiak. 2008. *Day-to-Day Assessment in the Reading Workshop: Making Informed Instructional Decisions in Grades 3–6.* New York: Scholastic.

Stead, Tony. 2004. *Reality Checks: Teaching Reading Comprehension with Nonfiction, K–5.* Portsmouth, NH: Stenhouse.

Walker, Rob. 2019. *The Art of Noticing: 131 Ways to Spark Creativity, Find Inspiration, and Discover Joy in the Everyday.* New York: Knopf.

Weissman, Elissa Brent, ed. 2018. *Our Story Begins: Your Favorite Authors and Illustrators Share Fun, Inspiring, and Occasionally Ridiculous Things They Wrote and Drew as Kids.* New York: *Simon & Schuster.*

Williams, Jennifer. 2017. "5 Steps to Build a Diverse Classroom Library and Encourage Empathy." *Global Learning* (blog), *Education Week*, September 6. http://blogs.edweek.org/edweek/global_learning/2017/09/5_steps_to_build_a_diverse_classroom_library_and_encourage_empathy.html.

Winfrey, Oprah. 2002. "Who Mentored Oprah Winfrey?" An interview with Oprah Winfrey on WCVB-TV 5 News (Boston) *CityLine*, January 13.

Yang, Gene Luen. 2016. "Reading Without Walls Challenge." https://read.macmillan.com/mcpg/reading-without-walls.

Zimmerman, Alycia. 2018. "Getting to Know My Students as Readers." *Top Teaching Blog*, August 24. www.scholastic.com/teachers/blog-posts/alycia-zimmerman/getting-know-my-students-readers.